IMMORTALITY

immortality

David Fairhurst

Amalgamated Memories
New York

Immortality
Copyright © 2013 by David Fairhurst
Immortality: A Comedy of Existential Dread
Copyright © 2004 by David Fairhurst
Immortality: An Original Screenplay
Copyright © 1991 by David Fairhurst

Published by Amalgamated Memories
Brooklyn, New York

CAUTION: Professionals and amateurs are hereby warned that *Immortality: A Comedy of Existential Dread* and *Immortality: An Original Screenplay* are subject to a royalty. They are fully protected under the copyright laws of the United States of America, and of all countries covered by the International Copyright Union (including the Dominion of Canada and the rest of the British Commonwealth), and of all countries covered by the Pan-American Copyright Convention and the Universal Copyright Convention, and of all countries with which the United States has reciprocal copyright relations. All rights, including professional and amateur stage performing, motion picture, recitation, lecturing, public reading, radio broadcasting, television, video or sound taping, all other forms of mechanical or electronic reproduction, such as information storage and retrieval systems and photocopying, and the rights of translation into foreign languages, are strictly reserved.

Inquiries concerning all rights should be addressed to the author at
david.fairhurst@gmail.com

All rights reserved.
No part of this book may be reproduced or transmitted in
any form or by any means, electronic or mechanical, including photocopying,
recording, or by any information storage and retrieval system,
without permission in writing from the author.

Library of Congress Control Number: 2013916644
ISBN-13: 978-0-615-88401-1
ISBN-10: 0-615-88401-6

Printed in the United States of America
Designed by David Fairhurst

10 9 8 7 6 5 4 3 2 1

First Edition

CONTENTS

Preface   vii

Immortality: A Comedy of Existential Dread   1

Immortality: An Original Screenplay   57

PREFACE

I've wanted to be a writer for nearly as long as I've been a reader, and in my early teens I started keeping a writer's notebook—a collection of ideas, fragments, bits of dialogue, and funny or thought-provoking quotes cribbed from real writers.

As a film fanatic in my mid-20s, I decided to combine my passions and give screenwriting a try. My first two scripts were based on actual events, but I had no luck selling them. (I did, however, recognize a good idea when I saw one, as both stories eventually became movies by other writers.) My next screenplay was a modern adaptation of an old Irish play, but Hollywood responded with a yawn.

Trying to figure out what the industry wanted was frustrating and futile, so for my next script I chose to write something personal, regardless of its commercial appeal. A few years earlier, I'd had the idea of a semiautobiographical film stitched together from the stuff in my notebook—which at this point had grown to four notebooks, each 200 pages long. I had no idea what the plot would be, but now was the time to find out.

So I went through my notebooks, copied every entry that seemed promising onto an index card (this was around 1988 and I didn't own a computer), then organized the cards thematically. Next, I tried to piece together a story.

Two years later, I had a handwritten 400-page monstrosity called *Swamp*, which I cut to 120 pages and retitled *Immortality*, a dark, unorthodox, Woody Allen-meets-Fellini-meets-*Taxi Driver* drama. (Hacking away those 280 pages is what taught me how to edit.) Nearly everyone who read it seemed to like it, but it wasn't exactly what Hollywood wanted.

I made one more stab at screenwriting—my goal this time was to write the most commercial script I was capable of without losing my self-respect—but by the time it was finished (in 1992), my heart had gone out of screenwriting. I was tired of toiling in the shadows. I wanted to be an actor.

I moved to New York in 1997, earned an MFA in acting in 2000, started booking jobs, and quickly discovered how difficult it is to sustain an acting career. But then I had an idea. A few years earlier I'd tried turning *Immortality* into a play, but now, with my acting career on the skids, I thought it might work as a one-man show and (not incidentally) a way to promote myself as an actor.

The screenplay relies heavily on voiceover, so turning it into a solo show seemed straightforward. What I quickly discovered, however, is that cinematic voiceover has a one-on-one intimacy that gets lost (or worse, sounds silly and pretentious) when you place the same words in the mouth of an actor talking to a live audience. So I was forced to cut much of the darkness (the Fellini-meets-*Taxi Driver* parts) and focus on the humor (the Woody Allen parts). The result is a very different script—sort of the standup-comedy version of *Immortality*. Originally I'd planned to publish only the one-man play, which I performed as part of the New York International Fringe Festival in 2004. But because it's so different, I decided to toss in the screenplay, too.

Reading them again after so long has been humbling. Having worked as an editor for the past decade, I recognize their flaws: the structural hiccups, jumbled themes, missed targets, hackneyed plotting, unmurdered darlings. At times I thought, "I can't publish these. It would be too embarrassing." Nevertheless, here they are. (I've resisted the urge to rewrite. Mostly.)

And one last thing: Given that *Immortality* is a first-person narrative by a character who shares my name—a device that sometimes causes readers to mistake fantasy for reality—I'm obliged to point out that these are works of imagination. The people, organizations, and events depicted are entirely fictitious.

Thanks for reading.

David Fairhurst
Brooklyn, N.Y.
September 2013

Immortality

A Comedy of Existential Dread

Immortality was first performed at the Paul Sharpe Gallery in New York City as part of the New York International Fringe Festival on August 15, 2004. It was directed by Lisa Deo and produced by Zenon Kruszelnicki.

CAST

DAVID	David Fairhurst
VOICES	Frank Biancamano
	Lisa Deo
	Colleen deVeer
	Jon Stuart Freeman
	Joan Porter Hollander
	Debbie Jaffe
	Brian Rhinehart
	Austin Sutcliffe

PRODUCTION NOTE

Only the actor playing David appears onstage, accompanied by recorded voices, sound effects, and slides projected on an upstage screen.

SCENE ONE

Lights up on a stage empty except for a single stool, on which sits DAVID, 40, who addresses the audience.

DAVID
I can't remember exactly when I decided I wanted to live forever, but I'm pretty sure it started in the fall of 1963. That's when two things happened. Number one...

> *SLIDE: John and Jackie Kennedy on the morning of their motorcade through Dallas.*

DAVID
...our long national summer of innocence finally came to an end.

> *The slide of John and Jackie fades to black.*

DAVID
And number two...

> *The sound of a gunshot.*

DAVID
...I was born.

> *SLIDE: A photo of DAVID as a baby.*

DAVID
Naturally, I blamed myself. Now, I'm not saying these two events were causally related—realistically, it's probably very unlikely that my birth caused the death of President Kennedy. But you gotta admit the timing is awfully suspicious, and my parents never let me forget it. It did make me the focus of all their attention, which I enjoyed, but I knew even that couldn't last...

The photo fades. The sound of a baby crying.

MOTHER
Come here and hold the baby!

BOY
I don't want to hold the baby!

SLIDE:

> **This is either an actual memory or a bit from an old TV show.**

FATHER
He says he doesn't want to hold the baby.

MOTHER
What do you mean he doesn't want to hold the baby?

BOY
I don't want to hold the baby!

MOTHER
What kind of person wouldn't want to hold this beautiful baby?

FATHER
If he doesn't want to hold the baby—

MOTHER
A person who'd kill our president in cold blood, that's who!

FATHER
For the last time, our son did not kill the president!

MOTHER
You gotta admit the timing is awfully suspicious.

FATHER
The Warren Commission didn't even mention his name!

MOTHER
Oh, the Warren Commission! The Warren Commission was a whitewash!

BOY
I don't want to hold the baby!

MOTHER
Tell me you love the baby!

BOY
No!

MOTHER
Say, "I love the baby!"

BOY
No!

MOTHER
Say, "I love you, little John-John"!

FATHER
You better do what she says, boy!

BOY
I love the baby! I love the baby!

DAVID
That wasn't the last lie I'd tell. And I think that's when I decided I wanted to be a writer: my first stab at immortality. After all, writers get paid to tell lies. And if the lies are good enough, your name will live forever, right? Besides, I've always believed that the truth is a precious commodity and should always be used sparingly....

SLIDE:

> Actually, that line was stolen from Mark Twain.

DAVID
So at the age of twelve I gave myself a pen name. My new name would be Richard Freeman: "Richard," derived from the Old High German word for "king"...

SLIDE:

> **These word derivations are entirely fictitious.**

DAVID
..."Freeman" from the Anglo-Saxon for a man released from bondage. Richard Freeman, King of Free Men, to emphasize the fact that even though my birth may have inadvertently killed a president, I still had free will! Unfortunately, I never actually got around to writing anything, but I gotta tell you, my autograph was a work of art....

> SLIDE: *A long column of "Richard Freeman" signatures in a child's unsteady hand.*

DAVID
Now, the reason I never wrote anything wasn't that I didn't have anything to say. On the contrary, I had way too much to say, especially when no one would listen. Thoughts would pop into my head like insects smacking the windshield of a car, leaving little black smudges all over my brain. Like a million voices inside my head, and they never shut up. Sometimes I'd have to

turn on the TV just to drown them out. Trying to write it all down would be futile.... It's just that, I don't want death to be the end of me, you know? I want to create something that'll live on after I die. Everybody wants to leave a mark on the world. I don't want to leave a mark. I want to leave a scar, you know, something permanent. Tangible proof that I, at one time, existed. And that's what I would obsess about every night, sitting in front of the TV and realizing that second by second, with every beat of my heart, my life was ticking away like a bomb. I'm forty years old and I've accomplished nothing. Imagine how much I could have accomplished in those forty years if I'd really set my mind to it. By the time Mozart was my age, he was already dead...

> SLIDE: *Wolfgang Amadeus Mozart (1756–1791)*
>
> DAVID *says the following names in rapid-fire succession, and simultaneously a slide with an image of the deceased and his or her dates appears for a second and then disappears.*

DAVID
Alexander the Great: dead...

> SLIDE: *Alexander the Great (356–323 B.C.)*

DAVID
Jesus: dead...

> SLIDE: *Jesus Christ (c.6 B.C.–c.30)*

DAVID
Martin Luther King: dead...

> SLIDE: *Martin Luther King (1929–1968)*

IMMORTALITY 9

DAVID

John Lennon: dead...

>SLIDE: *John Lennon (1940–1980)*

DAVID

George Gershwin: dead...

>SLIDE: *George Gershwin (1898–1937)*

DAVID

All five Brontë sisters: dead...

>SLIDE: *Charlotte Brontë (1816–1855)*

DAVID

...dead...

>SLIDE: *Emily Brontë (1818–1848)*

DAVID

...dead...

>SLIDE: *Anne Brontë (1820–1849)*

DAVID

...dead...

>SLIDE: *Maria Brontë (1814–1825)*

DAVID

...and dead.

>SLIDE: "*Elizabeth Brontë (1815–1825). Photo not available.*"

                    DAVID
James Dean: dead...

    SLIDE: *James Dean (1931–1955)*

                    DAVID
Poe...

    SLIDE: *Edgar Allan Poe (1809–1849)*

                    DAVID
...van Gogh...

    SLIDE: *Vincent van Gogh (1853–1890)*

                    DAVID
...Monroe: all dead...

    SLIDE: *Marilyn Monroe (1926–1962)*

                    DAVID
F. Scott Fitzgerald: almost dead...

    SLIDE: *F. Scott Fitzgerald (1896–1940)*

                    DAVID
Elvis: pretty much dead...

    SLIDE: *Elvis Presley (1935–1977)*

                    DAVID
Shakespeare...

    SLIDE: *William Shakespeare (1564–1616)*

DAVID
...not dead, but with *Hamlet*, *Julius Caesar*, *Othello*, and twenty-five other plays already under his belt. Woody Allen...

SLIDE: *Woody Allen (1935–)*

DAVID
...also not dead, but by the time he was my age, he had already stopped making funny movies. Now, I know what you're thinking. You're thinking, forty's not that old, you still have plenty of time left. But, come on, how do *you* know? Life is so fucking fragile. There's no guarantee any of us will be here tomorrow. You want to hear an interesting statistic? One out of every thirty people will die unexpectedly in the coming year.
   (pause, as he looks around the audience)
That's right. And the other twenty-nine don't think it'll be them either.

Light/music cue.

SLIDE:

> Always remember, you are unique.
> Just like everyone else.

SCENE TWO

Lights up. The previous slide fades out.

DAVID

So I grew up and moved to New York, now more desperate than ever to make my mark as a famous writer and live forever. I would try to write late at night, on the theory that that's when there would be less competition for all the good ideas. But it didn't work, because I still found it so much easier to just steal other people's lines and imagine that I'd written them.

SLIDE:

> "I like to write late at night when there's less competition for all the good ideas."
> —Randall Jarrell

DAVID

In fact, it didn't take me long to figure out the sad truth: that I *hate* writing. I hate everything about it. It's torture and I'm no good at it. It would have been nice to have discovered this sooner, but, you know, come on, I was busy!

> SLIDE: *The long line of "Richard Freeman" autographs seen earlier.*

DAVID

Writing is just one more item on the long list of things I can't do. For example, I can't hit a curveball....

> SLIDE: *DAVID, about ten years old, holding a bat and wearing a Little League uniform and a ridiculously oversized helmet.*

DAVID

I can't hit a fastball. I can't hit a—well, let's just say I can't hit a ball, period. Or catch a ball. Or throw a ball. Or kick a ball. Pretty much anything having to do with balls is out. I can't do that thing people do with their tongues, you know, curl it up into a little tube. Everyone can do that except me. I can't make an F chord on the guitar. I once tried to teach myself how to play, right? I had this idyllic vision of myself sitting casually on the floor of my funky East Village apartment, strumming on a guitar and singing to a small group of appreciative, pot-smoking friends.... But then you find out about all these stupid chords you have to learn! It's too much work! I can't even throw a Frisbee. I have this recurring nightmare that I'm walking down the sidewalk and a Frisbee lands at my feet and a group of kids in a field are shouting and waving at me to throw it back to them...

> *The faint sound of shouting children.*

DAVID

...so I pick it up and try to throw it, but it just flops over like a wounded duck and rolls away, and all the kids laugh at me with this contemptuous, jeering sound that instantly puts me right back in gym class trying to climb the rope. Or even worse—even worse than laughter and ridicule—is when they try to cheer you on with that phony inspirational pity they usually reserve for the retarded kid—you know, "Come on, David, you can do it!".... In my own defense, however, I must admit there is one unique skill I do possess: I have the uncanny ability to shake exactly two aspirin out of a bottle on the first try. Watch...

A drumroll. DAVID pulls out a bottle of aspirin and, with the dexterity of a magician, shakes two tablets into his palm and displays them to the audience.

DAVID

Thank you. This is the part of the show where the audience usually applauds, but don't feel any pressure.

Or, if the audience does applaud, improvise a line.

Light cue.

Music from a glossy, promotional, 1950s-style documentary trumpeting the achievements of hard-working white people.

NARRATOR

Today's young people are making it big as never before. In an age of unprecedented opportunity, they're on the fast track to wealth and success. All it takes is a little hustle and the proper can-do attitude.

DAVID

Deep down I knew I would never be a writer, but the alternative was just too horrible to contemplate: having to dress up in a suit and tie and convey the proper can-do attitude. Even at forty, I still feel like an imposter when I'm wearing a suit—like I'm eight years old, it's Halloween, and I'm going trick-or-treating dressed as my father. Like some guy with a badge is gonna tap on my shoulder and ask where my mommy and daddy are. Besides, stuck in an office all day with a bunch of spiteful, backstabbing coworkers—come on, that's not me. I'm an artist, man, I could never live like that. I'd just be miserable.... Kind of like the way I am now, except with health insurance.... So despite all evidence to the contrary, I clung to the illusion that a life of poverty and independence and artistic creation and pretending to be a writer was somehow ennobling. Yeah, well, that didn't last long. And it wasn't just my lack of talent—*everything* conspired against me.... And now, at this point in the show, I would like to do my one and only impression. This is my impression of the woman who lived directly above me in my very first New York City apartment.

> *DAVID stomps violently across the floor, jumps up and down on the floor, scrapes the stool loudly across the floor, etc.*

DAVID

Now, I could have lived with that. But when she opened up the bowling alley...

> *The sound of a bowling ball rumbling down an alley and smashing into pins.*

DAVID

(*Listening intently*) ...seven-ten split... (*To the audience*) ...which I'm pretty sure violated her lease, that's where I had to draw the line. So I moved to a new apartment and was immediately drawn into a battle with Bell Atlantic—I mean... Nynex? No, what was it then?... Verizon? I don't know. They keep changing their name, like a fugitive inventing new aliases, hoping to fool us into thinking they're a different company.... So at this time I was still trying to be a writer so I could live forever through my work, but instead I just lived forever on hold with the phone company. And the worst part about being on hold is not having to listen to the crappy music. No, the worst part about being on hold is when the song ends, and there's that pause, and your brain fools you into thinking that means someone's about to come on the phone, but then no, they just play another song!

   SLIDE:

> On hold, no one can hear you scream.

DAVID
So anyway, the reason I was calling was to get my phone number changed because the number they gave me—I swear to God—was one digit away from the number of the Suicide Prevention Hotline. And frankly, I just couldn't take it anymore: the nonstop calls at 4 o'clock in the morning from these desperate, lonely people. And the worst part about it is, I can't tell these people they have the wrong number: That could be the final thing that pushes them over the edge! I couldn't live with the guilt. So instead I'd just sit there and listen, for hours on end. You'd think that hearing all these tales of misery might actually make me feel better about my own life, but no, it doesn't work that way. Instead it makes me want to kill *myself* just to get off the damn phone!... When I couldn't take it anymore, I'd go to the movies. Spend the whole night there. Movie theaters have always been my refuge from the world. You know

how people always say they can remember exactly where they were when Kennedy was shot, or the space shuttle exploded? But what I remember just as vividly is the first moment I saw John Nance stab the mutant baby monster in *Eraserhead*.

    SLIDE: *John Nance in* Eraserhead.

DAVID

I remember exactly where I was, and what I was wearing, and what I had for dinner that night. Everything I know about life I learned at the movies. I mean, think about it: If a picture is worth a thousand words and a movie goes by at 24 frames per second, then a movie is worth... uh, wait.

    He tries to do the calculations in his head.

Twenty-four divided by—oh, shit, I can't do the math, but trust me, it's a lot of words.... I've wasted a lifetime sitting in darkened theaters watching other people's dreams unfold across the screen and imagining they're my own. Stealing other people's lines. When I really should've been at home, putting my own dreams down on paper. The paper itself becomes my enemy. The pressure of all those blank pages! That white void begging me to fill it. Every night those blank sheets would haunt me like ghosts. I'd find any excuse not to face them. Anything. I am never more creative than when I'm trying to find excuses not to write. I am the world's most accomplished procrastinator. For example, I'll sharpen every single one of my pencils until they're so sharp you could do surgery with them. I'll comb the bristles of my toothbrush. I'll straighten all the fringe on my carpet so that every strand is pointed in exactly the same direction. I'll rearrange all the shirts in my closet by color. Untangling the phone cord!—that's a good one. I'll try to figure out if a person caught in a rainstorm gets wetter if he walks or runs to his destination. I'll separate all my garbage into recyclables and nonrecyclables, going so far as to tear off the little plastic window from used envelopes so I can put it in the plastic bin instead of the paper bin. And how's this for irony? One of my all-time favorite ways to avoid work is to make to-do lists. And not just ordinary to-do lists. No, sir, I'm talking endless, multi-page nested hierarchies—things Microsoft Excel can't even do. I love making to-do lists. It creates the illusion that I'm accomplishing something. The only thing I love more than making to-do lists is crossing things off my to-do list. In fact, sometimes I'll put something on my to-do list that I've already done just so I can have the pleasure of crossing it off! Of course, I rarely get to cross anything off because I waste all my time making the damn to-do lists. But as good as I am at making to-do lists, there's one thing that trumps even that in my effort to avoid writing... and that's cleaning. My number-one method of procrastination. No one cleans like I do. Everywhere and everything. The top edges of my closet doors? Spotless. Beneath the stove, okay? Everywhere! When I get into that cleaning zone, cleaning becomes the sole focus of my existence, even though intellectually I know it's futile. I know we live in a chaotic, unpredictable universe, where cosmic forces beyond our control twist and shred vast reaches of space and matter, where people die without warning every single day, and no matter how many times I scrub the floor of my bathroom, it's still just one piece of a random universe. There's no cleanser in the world that's gonna change that. But still I'm powerless against the irresistible force of procrastination. In fact, I'm such a procrastinator *now*, can you imagine what I'd be like if I were *immortal*? I mean, *literally* immortal. So instead of saying, "Nah, I'll do that tomorrow," I could say, "Nah, I'll do that a million *years* from tomorrow." And then when the million years are up, I could still say, "You know, there's a really good show on TV tonight. I think I'll put it off for another million." If I were immortal, I would never get *anything* done! The prospect of my own death is the only reason I do anything. I swear to God, if it weren't for death, I would never move from the couch.... But after all this procrastinating and never writing a word, I just get so fucking depressed, I want to kill myself.... And I *would* kill myself, except I'm such a procrastinator! And then there's the prospect of having to write a suicide note! Oh my God, *writing* was the thing I was trying to avoid! The pressure of having to sum up all the reasons for ending my life for the benefit of future generations—I couldn't face it. I mean, I write a grocery list and go through twelve drafts—can you imagine me trying to write a damn suicide note? I do remember this one time, though, I was—I don't know, I was in a particularly good mood for some reason, and I just got this burst of energy, and I decided, That's it! I'm tired of being this way. I'm gonna turn over a new leaf. No more procrastinating! I'm finally gonna buckle down and write that suicide note! So I sat down to write it, but it just kept getting longer and longer, and by the time I hit 300 pages—and that was just the section dealing with my mother—and I'm sitting there waiting for the spell-check to finish, I was like, Oh, screw this, I'd rather live.

SLIDE:

Light/music cue.

SCENE THREE

Lights up.

DAVID

Does anybody have any questions about what we've covered so far? No? Okay.

SLIDE: *David's MOTHER.*

DAVID

My mother was a clinging, manipulative woman. She clung to my father and manipulated me and became the sun around which our small, hysterical universe revolved. My father's job in the household was to keep the peace between my mother and all the people who got on her nerves. My job was to be happy and normal.... Now, my father was very good at his job, and my mother grew to resent how dependent she was on him. But she never mentioned it, not once in twenty years. Never said a word. And for twenty years she patiently laid out his clothes on the bed every morning before he went to work, exactly the same every day: The gray suit. The white shirt. The blue tie. And two socks, one red and one green. And my father, color-blind since birth, never caught on.... When he died in the winter of 1978, my mother had his body cremated and sprinkled his ashes on the sidewalk in front of our house. To melt the ice. She said, "I always knew someday he'd make himself useful".... When we came home from the funeral, it was just the two of us in the house, and I knew, from that moment on, that *I* would be the one she clung to.... And she turned to me, and she lifted the black veil over her head, and she smiled sadly, and she said, "You're the man now, David. You're the man." And then she turned to Popeye, our two-year-old calico, and she said, "You're the cat now, Popeye. You're the cat."

(pause)

Actually, I stole that last part from a book.

> SLIDE: *The jacket cover of* Barrel Fever *by David Sedaris.*

DAVID
In truth, we didn't even have a cat. And all of my childhood memories are adulterated with lines I've stolen from real writers who know how not to procrastinate.

> SLIDE: *The face of David's* MOTHER, *with her shameless middle-class self-assurance.* DAVID *puts a telephone to his ear. His* MOTHER *speaks without pausing for a response.*

MOTHER
David? Is that you? I hardly recognize your voice anymore—you never call. So what have you been doing? Are you still trying to be a writer? I can't imagine there's much money in that. Is there? David? And I bet you're still living in that tiny apartment, too. Honestly, I don't know how you can live like that. You're like a savage. Do you need money? If you need money, I'm sure your Uncle Ron would let you borrow some.

DAVID
(overlapping)
No, I don't—

MOTHER
Maybe if you got a better job you could afford to live someplace nicer. Hmm? Don't you think? Why don't you ask your Uncle Ron if he has any nice jobs for you? I'm sure he wouldn't mind.

DAVID
(overlapping)
No, I really don't need—

MOTHER

I know! Why don't you take a computer class? I hear that's where the big money is. Do you want me to send you that article? I cut it out for you. I know it's not what you're interested in, but you can't always get what you want in life. You'll have to learn that someday. Don't you think? You're not getting any younger. I don't see why you don't ask Uncle Ron for a job. Do you want me to give you his number?

DAVID
(overlapping)

No, I—

MOTHER

I bet you don't even have his number.... David, what's wrong?

DAVID

What?

MOTHER

You sighed.

DAVID

No, I—

MOTHER

You did. I heard you.

DAVID

I—

MOTHER

What's wrong?

DAVID
Noth—

MOTHER
Then why did you sigh? You don't want to call him?

DAVID
I'll call him.

MOTHER
Do you want me to call him for you?

DAVID
I said I'll call him.

MOTHER
I know you won't call him. I'll call him for you.... Do you remember Steve Feldman? You know, he married Shirley's second cousin? The one who stuttered? The one from Pittsburgh? The one everyone thought was gay? You remember, don't you?

DAVID
(lying)
Oh, yeah, right, Steve Feldman.

MOTHER
Well, he just had a massive heart attack. Forty-two years old. Can you believe that? Shirley said his arteries were like peanut butter, that's how clogged he was. Just like that and he was gone. Isn't that amazing? David? I said, isn't that amazing?

DAVID
(overlapping)
Amazing.

MOTHER

So what kind of things do you write about? I know! Why don't you write a story about your cousin Mark? You know, the one who lost his arm in a boating accident? The one who became a banker? He's *very* successful. That would be an interesting story, don't you think? David? I really think you spend too much time alone. Do you have a girlfriend? What happened to that Kathy girl? She was nice. What's wrong? Don't you like girls? Don't you even *want* a girlfriend? Do you like wearing your hair that way? I'm just asking. The styles change, you know. Maybe that's why you don't have a girlfriend. Did you ever think of that? David? Did you ever think of that?

Her voice and image gradually fade.

DAVID

Talking to my mother is like going in for surgery with a doctor who won't stop poking at things until he figures out what's wrong with you.... But she was right that I needed to find a job. I couldn't survive any longer on my income from pretending to be a writer. So even though my resume lists so many short-term jobs it's starting to look like a rap sheet, I was determined to find a high-paying position that would finance my quest for immortality. I knew it wouldn't be easy and I'd need to get an early start, so every day I'd purposely set my clock fifteen minutes fast. Which, when you think about it, makes absolutely no sense. Because every morning I'd wake up, look at the clock, and go, "Okay, I know it's fifteen minutes fast, but I've already hit the snooze button twice, so uh, nine minutes times two, plus fifteen...," forcing myself, first thing in the morning, to do math in my head... which does not put me in a good mood. So I struggled for months to find a job that would support my goal of living forever. And I gotta tell you, jobs like that are not so easy to find.... At one point, I actually considered turning to a life of crime. Bank robbery, especially, has always appealed to me. There's a certain romanticism about it, and the best part is: The place is insured. It says so *right on the front door!* "Your money is federally insured." That's like an invitation to conscientious bank robbers. I rationalized it this way: If I get away with it, I'm rich, I don't have to work anymore, and I can spend all my time writing. If I *don't* get away with it, I go to prison, I don't have to work anymore, and I can spend all my time writing. You see? Either way, I come out ahead. And prison wouldn't be so bad, would it? Free food, free clothing, a roof over your head, and all the free time a man could ever want. My God, it's almost like winning the lottery. My prison fantasy: I'd spend all day working on the Great American Novel. At night I could finally read all the great books I keep telling myself I'll read someday when I get some free time—you know, Proust and Tolstoy and Dostoyevsky. My God, I haven't had free time like that since I had recess! That's what prison's gonna be for me—Dave's Classic Book Club! You see, if you approach it with the right frame of mine, prison could almost be a utopia. I mean, if you ignore the forced anal sex…. So that's the solution: Get myself arrested and then I can finally relax…. But come on. Who am I kidding? Rob a bank? Me? Once, I went to an ATM to withdraw $20, but instead of giving me one bill, the machine spits out two, but only debits my account for one. And I swear to God, I felt like Al Capone. And then, to make matters worse, the machine starts flashing me a message.

> SLIDE: *The screen of an ATM with the message "Do you want another transaction?"*

DAVID
And I thought, "Hmm… why not? Let's try it again." Like it's a slot machine, you know? Greed and guilt are at war inside me. But then I decided, "No, don't press your luck. Just pocket the money and go." But still, the guilt I felt for the rest of the week almost drove me to convert to Catholicism for the sole purpose

of going to confession.... I can't help it. I was born feeling guilty. Ever since my birth accidentally killed President Kennedy. Like whenever I hear about some horrific crime on the news and they don't know who did it, I can't help thinking, Well, maybe it was me. Maybe I did it and just don't remember. I mean, what if I have a split personality? What if I'm leading a double life I'm not even aware of? It would explain a lot—I mean, maybe that's why I'm so tired every morning.... Have you ever been walking down the sidewalk and somebody stops you and asks for directions, so you tell them how to get wherever they're going, but then, like a minute later, you suddenly realize, "Oh my God, I gave them the wrong directions"? So for the rest of the day, I'm worried I'm gonna run into this guy again, like he's gonna be looking for me....

MAN
Hey! You're the guy who gave me the wrong directions! Come back here!

DAVID
I'm so paranoid, I can't even talk to cross-eyed people. They always seem like they're up to something. It makes me nervous to have one eye looking at me and the other one looking over my shoulder. The problem with talking to cross-eyed people is you can't focus on both eyes at the same time. You gotta pick the one eye that's looking at you. So you're talking to the eye that's looking at you, right? And you're talking and talking, and then suddenly you realize, "Oh my God, now *this* eye's looking at me! And now *that* one's looking over my shoulder!"... Paranoia may be a healthy attitude when you live in New York, but even that's not gonna keep you alive forever. I remember hearing about a woman who was walking down the sidewalk and a falling girder lands on her head and kills her. How can you prepare for that? Or a normal, healthy person gets a brain aneurysm for no reason and drops dead without warning. We all

stand on the brink of death every single moment of our lives. How can a person live with that knowledge and not go insane? How can you live knowing you may never get to tell your story to the world? Everyone has a story to tell. There are six billion stories on earth, and not one of them will have a happy ending....

Overlapping VOICES, documentary-style.

MAN #1
I killed many human beings on the orders of my government....

WOMAN #1
We never talked in my family. We just taped Ann Landers columns to the refrigerator....

MAN #2
It's so hot. It never used to be this hot. The weather's been acting strange ever since they took them rocks off the moon....

WOMAN #2
Every man in my life has abandoned me. I can feel the world spinning under my feet....

MAN #3
Everywhere I turn, couples holding hands, laughing and talking, completely ignoring me....

MAN #4
I can't take this daily grind anymore. I want to tell my boss exactly what I think of him....

WOMAN #4
I want to buy a farm in Maine and make it a home for abandoned dogs....

MAN #5
I want to start my own religion....

WOMAN #5
I just want to catch the first bus whose destination is "away"....

MAN #6
I want to kill the rich and famous and feed them to the homeless....

DAVID
How can I expect the future to hear and remember my voice above the sound of all the others? You can't rely on the future. The future has been such a disappointment, hasn't it? When I was a kid, the future was filled with possibilities: flying cars and jet packs and robot maids—what happened to my robot maid? I want my robot maid! Now the future just sits out there, mocking me. No, you can't trust the future. I mean, think about it. *We* used to *be* the future—you and I. All those musty old writers who lived hundreds of years ago—all those Renaissance poets and Romantic novelists nobody reads anymore—they were counting on us to preserve their legacy. *Us.* I mean, what the hell were they thinking? We can't even figure out how to keep bananas fresh for more than five minutes. You buy them in the supermarket, they're green; by the time you get them home, they're brown. They're yellow for about two seconds, in the car, on the way home. You gotta pull over to the side of the road and eat them right there. If we can't even preserve bananas, how the hell are we gonna preserve *art*?

Light/music cue.

SLIDE:

The future is not what it used to be.

SCENE FOUR

Lights up.

DAVID
Eventually I came to the conclusion that I was never going to achieve immortality through my writing. So instead I decided to do it the old-fashioned way: by not dying.

SLIDE:

> Line stolen from a Woody Allen stand-up routine, circa 1968.

DAVID
I undertook a crash course in health and fitness. I made myself an expert on the function and dysfunction of the human body. Now, I've never worked out a day in my life, as you can plainly see: I have the body of a heroin-addicted British rock star from the '70s. I should be on an album cover wearing leather pants going like this....

SLIDE: DAVID on an album cover posed like a '70s British rock star.

DAVID

I swear to God, David Bowie could kick my ass. You see, I don't believe in exercise, never have. Unless you count pacing. And worrying. I mean, if pacing and worrying were an Olympic event, I would be captain of the American pacing-and-worrying team competing for the gold in Athens right now, but I don't think it really counts as exercise. No, I believe your heart has only so many beats in it, and once you've used them all, that's it, you drop dead. So why would I want to speed them up? If I wanted my heart to beat faster, I'd just drink stronger coffee. Despite this, however, everything I'd read said I should exercise to live longer, so I gave it a valiant effort. But no, it was hopeless, because I quickly discovered that I am literally allergic to fitness. Seriously. Whenever I tried to exercise, I would start sweating, and my breathing got labored, and my heart would race, and although I'm not a licensed physician, I know enough about medicine to recognize an allergic reaction when I see one. So I immediately quit exercising on the advice of, well, myself. Instead I decided to focus on nutrition and disease-prevention and everything else to extend my lifespan not involving exercise. I don't know if I extended my life by a single nanosecond, but there was one very important thing I did accomplish: I succeeded in turning myself into a world-class, Olympic-level hypochondriac. At least I *hope* I'm a hypochondriac. Because if I'm not, then that means I really am about to drop dead. I even bought this book...

SLIDE: The cover of The American Medical Association Complete Guide to Symptoms.

DAVID
...better known as "The Hypochondriac's Bible." According to this book, I've had everything. You name the disease, and at one time or another I've imagined I had it. In fact, here's an abridged list of just a few of the diseases I've thought I had over the years:

The screen shows an endless, quickly scrolling list of every disease known to man, plus a few known only to DAVID:

> ...whooping cough, astigmatism, shingles, warts, twitching, cold chills, hot flashes, West Nile virus, East Nile virus, swollen glands, fat lip, migraine, Lyme disease, Alzheimer's disease, SARS, bird flu, wheezing, sneezing, poor posture, excessive ear wax, public humiliation, pulmonary embolism, acne, shortness of breath, hysterical blindness, squinting, scoliosis, eczema, botulism, carpal tunnel syndrome, mongolism, hypothyroidism, cat-scratch fever, appendicitis, Lou Gehrig's disease, Lou Costello's disease, frozen shoulder, male pattern baldness, sleepwalking, German measles, pain in the neck, ringing in the ears, nosebleed, small pox, medium pox, extra large pox, dehydration, detached retina, heartburn, palpitations, abdominal swelling, meningitis, encephalitis, gastroenteritis, flat feet, can't stop sweating, seeing spots, chronic choking, absent-mindedness, discolored tongue, hiccups, blisters, blotches, food poisoning, myocardial infarction, anaphylactic shock, bad attitude, irritable colon, angry bowel, mad cow disease, jaundice, anemia, Parkinson's disease, inflamed gums, social anxiety, tuberculosis, something wrong with my pancreas, funny smell, hallucinations, dizziness, ears too big, seasickness, can't get a song out of my head...

DAVID
In high school, I had erectile dysfunction. I don't mean I couldn't get it up; I'm saying it wouldn't go down. I had an erection in high school that lasted four years. In college, I had a severe case of plagiarism.

SLIDE:

> "In college, I had a severe case of plagiarism."
> —line stolen from a book

DAVID

Once, I found some mold in my bathtub, and I'd read that long-term exposure to mold can affect your cognitive function, so I tested myself by watching *Jeopardy!*, and I got the Final Jeopardy question wrong five days in a row—and that *never* happened before—which proved that mold was eating my brain! My hypochondria was so severe I couldn't sleep, I couldn't get out of bed—I would just lie there, for hours, memorizing the pattern of cracks in my ceiling and listening to the beat of my own heart. And if you've ever paid really close attention to your own heartbeat, you know it's not entirely regular. Every now and then, between one beat and the next, there'll be a microscopically longer pause than usual, and every single one of those little extra pauses would literally drive me insane! And by "literally," I mean figuratively! And I would start obsessing over the mechanical function of my heart—like, for example, what is it that keeps your heart beating in the first place? Can anybody answer that? What makes it go? What's the power source? I mean, it doesn't have a battery. There's no electrical cord sticking out of your chest. It just seems to go all by itself. Well, if it just goes all by itself, then what's to prevent it from stopping all by itself? And thinking about that would give me chest pains, and my heart would start beating faster and louder. And sometimes, late at night, my heart would beat so loud, I was afraid the neighbors were gonna complain....

There's a sudden pounding on the wall.

MAN
Hey in there! Stop beating your heart so loud! We're trying to sleep!

DAVID
But the worst part about being a hypochondriac is *not* the constant anxiety over whether you've got stomach cancer or Lou Gehrig's disease, or imagining that every little twinge is the first subtle sign of the illness that's going to kill you. No, the worst part is knowing for a fact that someday, you're going to be right. I mean, we're all gonna die of something, right? So after all the false alarms, the meaningless MRIs, the patronizing doctors, finally you will be vindicated and they will actually find a fatal disease. That's what really stinks about being a hypochondriac: knowing that the first time you *finally* get it right... congratulations: You're dead.

BLACKOUT.

DAVID
(in darkness)
Oh my God, I've gone blind.

SLIDE:

IMMORTALITY 35

Scientific studies have shown that people who don't think about death live longer.

SCENE FIVE

Lights up.

DAVID

When you can't sleep, the night seems to race by so fast, and you watch the clock thinking, Okay, if I fall asleep right now, I'll still be able to get a good solid half an hour before I have to get up. Why would I want to sleep anyway? *I'm dying.* Little by little, cell by cell. It may not show up on an x-ray yet, but trust me, it's there. Who can afford to waste any time asleep? I might miss something good on TV.... I remember once I wasted several nights in a row creating a chart depicting how I've managed to waste most of my time over the past forty years and extrapolating it over the course of a lifetime....

> SLIDE: *A chart listing various activities and the amount of time spent on them over the course of a human lifespan:*

```
Page 7

156. Listening to drum solos...................35 days
        (see also Allman Brothers Band, p. 9)

157. Making to do lists......................104 days

158. Searching for the remote.................56 days

159. When eating in public, wondering
        whether the chewing sound outside
        my head is as loud as the chewing
        sound inside my head.....................13 days

160. Getting out of the shower because
        I thought I heard the phone ringing........2 days

161. Watching "Blind Date" and thinking
        why am I watching this?....................8 days
```

DAVID

Assuming I live an average human lifespan of seventy-eight years, by the time I die I will have spent approximately thirty-five days listening to drum solos, fifty-six days searching for the remote. When eating in public, wondering whether the chewing sound outside my head is as loud as the chewing sound inside my head: thirteen days!

The SLIDE fades out.

DAVID

And here's another one: Have you ever been watching a TV show that you taped but you forgot that you taped it, you think you're watching it live, and so you're sitting there watching the commercials, going, "Come on, come on, enough commercials," and then you suddenly remember, "Oh shit, I taped this, I can fast-forward, where's the remote?!," but then it's too late, the show comes back on, and you watched all those commercials for nothing? Well, welcome to every night of my life. I am the end result of everything I've seen on TV. My moral character was sculpted by the little homilies Robert Reed told at the end of every episode of *The Brady Bunch*. I yearned to live in a town where all of life's problems could be solved in half an hour, home to the good old-fashioned American values we all cherish on sitcoms but not so much in real life. And where, every Saturday morning, Wile E. Coyote died for your sins.... People on TV aren't obsessed with death. Why can't I be more like them? I keep asking myself, What's wrong with me? And I'm sure you all have an answer for that by now, but I'm not asking *you*, I'm asking *me*! What's wrong with me? Normal people don't obsess over their own mortality. They just grow up, get married, and have kids—biological immortality, right? When my mother was my age, her nest was already empty. Her kids had already grown up and moved out. I don't even have a nest. I can't believe I forgot to build a nest. What the hell was I thinking? Is it too late for me to build a nest? Could someone help me find some twigs or something? I don't even know *how* to build a nest. But that's what I have to do: Somehow I have to find a woman willing to bear my children, ensuring my legacy, my conquest of death... So, anyone know where I can find a woman?

> *Light cue. The sounds of a party: people talking, laughing, music playing, etc.*

DAVID

I *hate* parties. I should never go to parties. It's always a mistake. At every party I go to, the result is the same: me, standing near a wall, holding a glass, occasionally moving it to my lips in a simulation of drinking, lamely tapping my foot to the music in a pathetic attempt to look like a guy who's having a "good time," like that's gonna make me "fit in," despite the impenetrable *Star Trek*-like force field surrounding my body that prevents anyone from even noticing my presence—I swear to God, I'm so invisible at a party, I could actually rob the place and nobody would know. Every now and then I'll check my pocket to make sure I still have the list of clever things to say I copied out of magazines. At some point I'll cross the room so I can stand next to the potted plant and pretend to examine it, as if I'm casually taking a break from all the "fun" I've been having on the other side of the room. And I'll think, "Well, look at this fascinating plant. Fine leaves. Very shiny. I wonder how long I can stand here and pretend to be utterly absorbed by this plant."... Why do I feel like an extra in my own life? Like the main action of the story is going on someplace else, while I just stand here, filling in the background, without any lines to say.... No, parties are always a bad idea. And then there's all that pressure to dance. Oh my God. I can't dance. The only dance moves I know come from the *Charlie Brown Christmas* special. So while everyone else is dancing like a normal adult, I'm doing lots of this... and this...

> *He demonstrates dances from the* Charlie Brown Christmas *special.*

DAVID

...which is really not very attractive to women.... I guess the problem I have with parties is: I just don't understand the whole concept of "fun." I mean, I've seen pictures of people having fun. I can recognize it. I know what fun looks like. I just don't know how to do it. And it's not like I don't *like* other people. I *love* talking to people—I find it fascinating. I mean, you know, except for the part where you have to listen to the other person talk. And pretend to be interested in what they're saying—*that* I'm no good at.... But I kept telling myself, I have to do this. I have to go to this party and find a woman to bear my children. My whole future is at stake. So I gave myself a pep talk. I said, Okay, Dave, everything will be fine. You're all prepared. You've got your list of clever things to say. You're gonna have a great time. You just have to relax and be yourself.... And then it dawns on me: What the hell am I saying? "Relax and be myself"? Now there's an oxymoron.... You know that scene in every romantic comedy where the lonely but attractive protagonist can't find Mr. Right, and so the protagonist's quirky but not quite so attractive friend says something like...

MOTHER

You just haven't found the right person yet. I believe there's one special someone out there for everyone.

DAVID

...as if that's supposed to make her feel better. But when I hear a statement like that, what I think is, Okay, one special someone out there for everyone....

> SLIDE: *A sheet of paper containing the following scribbled calculations:*

```
  6,384,821,260      Total world population
                     (as of 8/6/04)
             ÷2
  3,192,410,630      Total women on earth
 -1,064,136,877      -33% too young
  2,128,273,753
   -709,424,584      -33% too old
  1,418,849,169
   -851,309,501      -60% already married
    567,539,668
   -425,654,751      -75% don't speak English
    141,884,917
     -7,094,246      -5% lesbians
    134,790,671      Total single, available,
                     age-appropriate, English-
                     speaking, heterosexual
                     women
        ÷365.25      Dates per year (including
                     one "leap date" every
                     four years)
        369,278      Maximum number of
                     years to find Miss Right
```

DAVID

So, there are six billion people in the world—that's three billion women. Subtract the ones who are too young or too old or too married or too lesbian or don't speak English and we're left with approximately 135 million single, available, age-appropriate, English-speaking, heterosexual women. Now, if I go out on a date with one woman a night, every night for the rest of my life, in order to find "the one," it should take me no more than... 369,278 years. Okay. But still, I'm not discouraged. Because, remember, this is just the theoretical maximum amount of time it *could* take me, assuming that after dating every single woman on earth, Miss Right turns out to be *the very last one*, and what are the odds of that happening? So realistically, I figure

I'm looking at no more than 100,000 years, tops.... Still, I should probably get started.

> SLIDE: *A photo of a smiling young woman, labeled "#000000001: Angela Aabgaard."*

DAVID
Number 1: Angela Aabgaard. Age thirty-two. Five-foot-six.... Now, I tried to approach this scientifically, like an anthropologist of the heart. For weeks ahead of time, I did research. I bought books about women. I studied their mating habits. I watched the Lifetime network. I memorized the rules for successful courtship.

VOICE
Number 1: Smile and make eye contact.

DAVID
Smile and make eye contact. No problem. As long as she's not cross-eyed, I'm good.

VOICE
Number 2: Ask questions and pretend to be interested in what she says. For example, "What do you do for a living?"

DAVID
So, what do you do for a living? Really? That's so interesting.

VOICE
Number 3: Compliment her appearance. For example, "That's a very pretty sweater you're wearing."

DAVID
That's a *very* pretty sweater you're wearing. That's a very *pretty* sweater you're wearing. That's a very pretty *sweater* you're wearing.... I came up with approximately 900 different ways to say,

"That's a very pretty sweater you're wearing," entered them on a spreadsheet, categorized and subdivided by mood, occasion, venue, lighting, type of sweater, color of sweater, and about 14 other categories, every single variation on the tip of my tongue, waiting for the perfect opportunity to be served up with my smooth, polished delivery.... Of course, if she's not wearing a sweater, then I'm screwed—I'll have absolutely nothing to talk about! Oh God, I was such a nervous wreck before our first date, I was actually relieved when she didn't show up....

The SLIDE of Angela Aabgaard fades out.

DAVID
But afterwards, it bothered me. I couldn't figure out what I did wrong. I went over every single detail of our initial conversation until I pinpointed the exact moment I scared her off, and I concluded it must have been when I said "hello." "Hello"?! What the hell was I thinking?! I should have said "hi"! "Hi"! Who says "hello" these days? I can't believe I said "hello"—like a *schoolmarm*!

SLIDE:

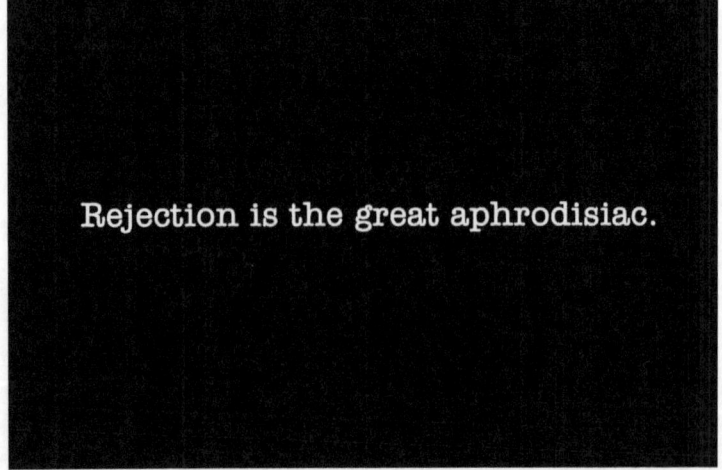

DAVID

I bet women never have these problems. They're like cats and we're like mice and they're just toying with us, batting us back and forth between their paws. And then they complain about equality with men! Equality with men? Are you kidding?! Women who want equality with men lack ambition.... But I knew I had to keep going out on dates until I found "the one." I was obsessed. Dating is like playing the lottery: You know you're never going to win, but you just keep on buying tickets.... And then there was Darcy Myers...

SLIDE: *Darcy Myers.*

DAVID

...a woman about as stable as Jell-O....

DARCY

...The fact that I can kill myself anytime is what keeps me alive. It's like my personal choice, you know? I used to be a very negative person, but then I started doing Pilates and I hardly felt suicidal at all. Jerry says I'm too hard on myself—that's my life coach, Jerry. Did I mention that I'm seeing a life coach? It's only three times a week, but at least it gets me out of the house. I used to be agoraphobic but now I'm the opposite of agoraphobic—do you know if there's a name for that? I should know—I mean, I *was* a psych major. Jerry says I became a psych major because I was looking for someone to blame. Is that funny? I really should have been a dancer, though—that's what everyone tells me: "Darcy, you should have been a dancer." Except no one's ever said that to me, I just made it up, but I think it would be fun, don't you? Maybe in my next life. Do you believe in reincarnation? Now, don't get me wrong, my cat is very special to me, but I think if I'm reincarnated, I'd rather come back as a sea otter.... If you don't want to go out with me again, that's okay. I mean, it's not like I'm still suicidal or anything.

DAVID

It was the greatest date of my life! She wouldn't let me get a word in, so there was no pressure for me to talk. Plus, her self-esteem was even lower than *mine*! Oh my God, I think I'm in love! You see, this should have been my strategy all along. I was being too clinical, searching for a smart, beautiful, confident woman who'd make a great mother for my children. But women like that are totally out of my league. Instead I should have been much more primal, thinking more like a lion stalking a herd of antelope. I should be picking out the slow ones, the weak, the sick, the stupid, the helpless, the ones who can't keep up with the herd—those are the women I can catch. In fact, as a general rule, I wish all of life were more like *Mutual of Omaha's Wild Kingdom*. That way all the dumb people would get eaten by lions. That's the problem with living at the top of the food chain: Eliminating the weak and the stupid and preventing them from reproducing is nature's way of strengthening the species, but since human beings have no natural enemies, the laws of evolution dictate that we're just going to keep getting dumber and dumber and dumber until every single last human being has accidentally locked himself inside his car and we all die of starvation. Wouldn't life be so much more interesting if, every single time you stepped out your door, there was a slight possibility that a giant predatory bird would swoop down, grab you in his claws, and carry you off for dinner? I seriously think they should consider releasing a few humans back into the wild. For example, like these people—how many times has this happened to you?

DAVID
(miming a phone conversation throughout)

The phone rings, right? You pick it up and say, "Hello?" And then there's a pause, and the person calling you says, "Hello?" You see, the problem now is we're at an impasse, and the only way to get out of this impasse is for me—because it's *my* turn now—is for me to again say, "Hello?" So now *I've* said hello, *he's* said hello, I've said hello a *second* time, we've exchanged a grand total of *three* hellos, and we've gotten absolutely *nowhere*! "I don't have time for this! Don't you realize I'm dying!" So here's what I like to do: The phone rings. I pick it up and say, "Hello?" I wait for the pause. The person calling me says, "Hello?" And then I say, "Yes, is Frank there? Frank? Yeah, can I talk to Frank, please? Oh, really? You don't know who Frank is? Hmm. That's funny. Well, maybe that's because *you're the one who called me, you moron!!*...

(to the audience)

So anyway, everything was going great with Darcy. Until one night, we were walking along the beach, and a giant predatory bird swooped out of the sky and carried her off...

The squawk of a giant predatory bird, and the SLIDE of Darcy Myers slowly fades.

Light/music cue.

SCENE SIX

Lights up.

DAVID

I had no religious upbringing as a child. Unless you count listening to the soundtrack to *Jesus Christ Superstar* over and over. So I've never believed in an afterlife. But I really wish I could, you know? That would solve all my problems.... Well, not *all* of them. I mean, not the ones I was *born* with, but you get the idea.... To believe that death is not the end of life but a transition to something better—whether heaven literally exists or not doesn't even matter. Just believing with all your heart that it does—that would be paradise on earth. And maybe they're right. No one knows for sure....

> *SLIDE: A page from the screenplay for the 1986 Woody Allen movie* Hannah and Her Sisters *containing the following lines, which DAVID quotes word for word:*

DAVID
...But for me, "maybe" is just not good enough. I want certainty or nothing. "Maybe" is just too, too slim a reed to hang my whole life on.... I've thought long and hard about this and—

> *DAVID notices the slide.*

DAVID
Okay, maybe *I* didn't think long and hard about this, but someone did.

> *The SLIDE fades out.*

DAVID
You see, I think death is like the time before you were born: You're nothing; you don't exist. But at least before you're born, you're not *aware* of the fact that you don't exist. When you're dying, you know exactly what's coming.

> *Light/music cue.*

DAVID
I thought I could live forever by having kids. Childbirth—one of life's most beautiful and disgusting miracles, all that noise and blood and screaming and that little writhing, wriggling creature from another planet all covered in putrid alien muck, I swear to God the whole thing looks like a Quentin Tarantino movie—

but as a form of immortality, it leaves a lot to be desired. Sure, your kids will remember you, your grandkids maybe, but once they're gone, there'll be no one left who remembers you. You might as well have never existed. No, I want to control my own destiny. I want to write myself into history, and that's a really hard book to get into. I want to be a part of something eternal. I want to tamper with the universe. I want to be on the FBI's Ten Most Wanted List so at least I'll be wanted by someone. *I want to have it all!* I mean, no, I want to get *away* from it all! No, wait—oh, shit, I don't know! All I do know is, maybe it *is* my destiny. Maybe my mother knew something when she blamed me for killing Kennedy. Achieving a level of fame great enough to assure your immortality is hard, but *killing* somebody famous... that's actually pretty easy. You know, I didn't want to think about this possibility, but it was always there in the back of my mind, as a last resort. So I studied the psychology of assassins. I read up on assassins throughout history. I went to the Broadway musical *Assassins*. I got this book that compared all the world's most famous assassins and figured out what they had in common. And that's when I made a startling discovery....

SLIDE:

Fig. 1: Common Characteristics of Assassins Throughout History: A Cross-Cultural Perspective

Gender: Male

Age range: 25–40

Race: Caucasian

Relationships: Few close friends or relatives.

Social skills: Often a troubled loner who has difficulty maintaining meaningful long-term relationships.

Beliefs/opinions: May be fanatically obsessed with a single issue.

DAVID

Male. Twenty-five to forty—I just made the cutoff. Caucasian. Few close friends or relatives—is this starting to sound like anyone you know? But wait, look at this one: "Often a troubled loner who has difficulty maintaining meaningful long-term relationships"—oh my God, has this guy been reading my diary or what?... Now, I realize this may be taking things to an extreme. But listen: How does that saying go? If a tree falls in the forest and no one hears it, does it make a sound? Well, if a person lives and dies and no one remembers him, was that person ever really alive at all?

SLIDE:

> Line stolen from the back cover of a self-help book.

DAVID

Look, I'll never be Shakespeare. I'll never be Einstein or Jesus or Elvis. Killing the president may be the only chance I have. There's a little voice inside my head that keeps telling me I have to do this. It's my destiny. And let's face it: If you can't trust the voices inside your own head, who *can* you trust?...

Light/music cue.

SLIDE:

> Better to be cursed than to be forgotten.

SCENE SEVEN

Lights up. The SLIDE fades out.

DAVID

Well, obviously I didn't kill the president. I made plans to, but then there was something on TV I wanted to watch that night. So I set the VCR to tape it, right? But then I realized, Wait a minute, if I kill the president tonight, there's a pretty good chance they're going to interrupt regularly scheduled programming with a special report and the show will be preempted. But if I stay home to watch the show, I'll miss my chance to kill the president. Logistically, it was just way too complicated. And besides: John Wilkes Booth, Lee Harvey Oswald, John Hinckley, nobodies who became somebodies by shooting the president— it's such a cliché. I have to think up something better than that.... But I gotta tell you, I was really looking forward to seeing myself on the news.

SLIDE: David's mug shot.

DAVID

Maybe then my life would have meaning. Maybe then people would finally take notice of me. People like Mrs. Stern, my third grade teacher. I spent an entire year in her class and she never once got my name right. She had this disgusting flab on the back of her arms and every time she wrote on the blackboard, it would flap back and forth, and no matter how hard I tried, I couldn't take my eyes off it—it was disgusting and mesmerizing at the same time—until finally she'd have to yell at me and say, "Daniel! Pay attention!" Or the kids at summer camp who wouldn't play with me. Every year my parents would ship me off to Camp Lord of the Flies, and I'd spend the entire summer locked in my cabin writing practice suicide notes. I was so anonymous, I didn't even merit a nickname, and none of my T-shirts said anything. But maybe if I were on TV, all of that would change. So that's what I had to do: Crash the celebrity-industrial complex. If I wanted to live forever, I had to become an actor and somehow get myself on TV.

Light/music cue.

DAVID
And now, finally, I'd like to present to you the successful end to my search for immortality, my ultimate conquest of death....

SLIDE: A photo of DAVID on Law & Order.

DAVID
Except I can't show you the actual clip, because if I do, NBC will sue me. But I watched it obsessively, and I think it was around the forty-seventh or forty-eighth time that I noticed something odd. Here, I'll demonstrate.... As I'm crossing in front of Jerry Orbach, I noticed that I do this:

He crosses the stage and makes a slight bob with his head.

DAVID
And the first time I saw it, I thought, What the hell was that? Why did I make that stupid move with my head?

He demonstrates again.

DAVID
So I watched it again. I watched it over and over. I watched it in slow motion. I watched it backwards. I watched it backwards in slow motion. I watched it frame by frame—it became my personal Zapruder film. And every single time, there it was.

He demonstrates again.

DAVID

And I thought, Oh my God! *That's* what I'm gonna be remembered for! *That's* my legacy! The guy playing the lab technician on *Law & Order* who makes that stupid head-bob move! There it is: I'm immortal.... You know, I shot that episode four years ago and they never invited me back... and now I know why!

Light/music cue. The SLIDE fades out.

SCENE EIGHT

Lights up. SLIDE: David's father.

DAVID

On the day I turned six years old, my father gave me the greatest birthday present any six-year-old could ever want: He took me to see a live appearance by the number-one television personality in my demographic: Bozo the Clown. Now, Bozo did a little magic show, and at one point he gazed out at the audience and picked three or four kids—and one parent—to come up on stage with him and be his assistants. And of all the parents in the crowd, the one he chose was my father. You know, I really envied the kids who got to be Bozo's assistants, but it didn't matter. I would have been too nervous anyway. But seeing my father up there, well, that was enough for me: I could not have been more proud of him. Now, Bozo would shuffle three coconut shells, and all my father had to do was pick the one with the hidden Ping-Pong ball. But no matter how hard he tried, my father could never get the right shell. Somehow Bozo made that ball jump from shell to shell as if by magic, and every time my father came up empty, the kids in the audience would laugh and laugh, louder and louder each time, until they were screaming with laughter, until the whole building trembled with their laughter, and I sat there alone and watched my father's face turn red. When he came down from the stage at last, he

grabbed my hand without saying a word and took me home....
That night, as I lay awake in bed, I could hear my father downstairs at the kitchen table. He was shuffling three overturned cereal bowls, trying to figure out how Bozo had done it. How Bozo the Clown had humiliated him in front of all those kids. For hours on end I could hear him down there, shuffling and reshuffling those bowls, desperately trying to learn the secret. But it was hopeless, and finally he gave up and went to bed.... And this may be hard to believe, but my father was never really the same after that. He had been the kind of man who never really thought deeply about things, you know? He was blessed with a simple faith that God was in heaven and all was right with the universe. But now, after the Bozo incident, his whole view of the world was shattered. It was 1968, and for my father, nothing ever made sense again: Bobby Kennedy. Martin Luther King. Vietnam. How could things ever make sense when we lived in a world like that, a world where people died for no reason, a world of cosmic absurdity where a clown—a kiddie show clown—could subvert the physical laws of reality?... Well, my father never did figure out the secret of Bozo's shell game. And about ten years later he died, a broken shell of a man....

The SLIDE of David's father fades out.

DAVID
And for the rest of my life, I've been haunted by the notion that, on what should have been the happiest day of my life, Bozo the Clown killed my father.... I guess life is full of disappointments. And I am full of life.... And every single word of this show has been true. And even if some of it wasn't true, that doesn't mean you shouldn't believe it. Because the plain and simple truth is... the truth is never plain or simple....

SLIDE:

> Line stolen from Oscar Wilde.

                    DAVID
And I still intend to live forever...

  SLIDE:

> Line stolen from Oscar Wilde.
> Dead at 46.

DAVID checks his pulse to make sure he still has one.

DAVID

...So far, so good.

BLACKOUT. Closing music.

Immortality

An Original Screenplay

AUTHOR'S NOTE

Like the play, the screenplay version of *Immortality* contains lines inspired by (or stolen from) writers far better than I, including Samuel Beckett, Tom Stoppard, and J.D. Salinger. I haven't referenced them here as I did in the play, however, mainly because I wrote this so long ago—about 1990—that I can't remember which are original and which are stolen. (With one exception: The character Amy Rosen, who first appears on Page 159, and several of her lines were improvised by Lew Schneider during a writing session of the University of Pennsylvania's Mask & Wig Club circa 1982.) I will attempt to give credit where it's due in future editions of this book.

FADE IN:

INT. A SUBWAY TRAIN - DAY

RICHARD FREEMAN, 29, an overeducated underachiever, sits on a crowded subway train with all his worldly possessions: a travel bag stuffed with clothes and a 13-inch television. Thin, pale, and haunted, he casts his gaze at the desperate faces of his fellow TRAVELERS, exploring the wrinkled landscapes of lives.

> RICHARD (V.O.)
> People in this city have a way of focusing their eyes about three feet in back of your head so it seems they're looking right through you.... It really annoyed me when I first moved here. Now, I think I'm getting the hang of it.

The lights flicker off and on; the subway SCREECHES to a stop.

EXT. A CITY SIDEWALK - DAY

On a gloomy day in late winter, Richard lugs his bag and TV set precariously down an icy sidewalk.

> RICHARD (V.O.)
> My name is Richard Freeman. "Richard" from the Old High German word for king, "Freeman" from the Anglo-Saxon "free man." Richard Freeman, King of Free Men... I made it up myself. I believe a self-made man should have a self-made name.

As Richard wearily mounts the steps of a rundown apartment building, a scrawny KID fires a snowball into the back of his neck and scampers away down the street, pointing and cackling diabolically.

INT. THE APARTMENT BUILDING - DAY

Leaning against the wall, Richard waits for the elevator.

> RICHARD (V.O.)
> Now I suppose you want to know all about me, like where I was born and how I ended up here and what I think about the president. And I could tell you. I could tell you the truth or I could make something up—it really doesn't make any difference. People believe what they want to believe. They're not interested in the truth. People just want to hear a good story.

INT. A STAIRWELL - DAY

Richard struggles up the stairs with his bag and television.

> RICHARD (V.O.)
> I was born in the summer of '63, the last American summer of innocence before the world fell apart. Kennedy, Oswald, Vietnam—nothing was ever the same again.... For that, I blame myself. Somehow my arrival at that particular moment in history altered the fabric of the universe.

EXT. A CITY STREET - DAY

Trapped behind the wheel of a rented Ford, hemmed in by gridlock on all sides, Richard tries desperately to squeeze through the door, but it's blocked by another car. As a timer on the dashboard hits 12:00, a tremendous EXPLOSION rocks the whole block and his car is consumed in a fireball.

INT. RICHARD'S APARTMENT - NIGHT

Richard's one-room apartment is barren, except for his TV in the center of the floor and a mattress against one wall. With a pad and a pen, he sits on the mattress, trying to write, surrounded by crumpled-up sheets of paper.

> RICHARD (V.O.)
> I guess you could say I'm a born liar. Maybe that's why I write. A writer, after all, is a professional liar. Writers tell lies and get paid for it. Lies in the service of truth.... It's very confusing. But a little honesty goes a long way. I believe the truth is a precious possession and should always be used sparingly.... Even as a kid, I wanted to be a famous writer, though I didn't actually write much....

INT. YOUNG RICHARD'S BEDROOM - NIGHT

A 12-YEAR-OLD RICHARD sits at his desk with a stack of library books, inscribing them all to imaginary admirers and signing his autograph on the title page.

INT. RICHARD'S APARTMENT - NIGHT

Richard signs his name over and over on the pad, then tears off the sheet and tosses it away. Mindlessly he flicks on the TV, bathing the room in a mystical glow.

> RICHARD (V.O.) (cont.)
> It wasn't that I didn't have anything to say.

> My mind is a jumble of words and thoughts, all clamoring for attention, like a million voices inside my head, and they never shut up. Never. I have no control over my own thoughts. They pop into my brain like insects smacking the windshield of a car, leaving a little black smudge on my psyche. Sometimes they keep me awake at night. Sometimes I have to turn on the TV just to switch off those clamoring voices. And sometimes even then....

Suddenly, from out of the shadows, TRAVIS appears. Seen in the shimmering light of the TV, he's Richard's manic alter ego. Travis leafs through some of Richard's papers, then commences a rapid-fire litany of dread.

TRAVIS
Why do you do this stuff, Dave? Why are you killing yourself?

RICHARD
I have a thing about immortality.

TRAVIS
But it's pointless. Nobody reads anymore. Reading takes too long...

RICHARD
I want to create something that'll live on after I die.

TRAVIS
...This is the post-literate age. People today rent videos—they want to see blood, exploding cars...

RICHARD
I want people to know who I am.

TRAVIS
...Words eventually fade away, but scar tissue is forever.

RICHARD
I don't want death to be the end of me.

TRAVIS
Death is the end of everyone, Dave.

RICHARD
Stop calling me Dave. Dave is dead.

TRAVIS
There are five billion stories on earth and not one will have a happy ending. Second by second, your life is ticking away like a bomb.

RICHARD
I've accomplished nothing in twenty-nine years.

TRAVIS
Imagine how much you could have accomplished...

RICHARD
If only I had those years to live over...

TRAVIS
By the time James Dean was your age, he was dead.

RICHARD
If only I'd been born yesterday and all of this was a dream.

TRAVIS
How do you know you'll even be here tomorrow? One out of every thirty people in the world will die unexpectedly this year, and you know what? The other twenty-nine don't think it'll be them either.

RICHARD
I can't imagine myself being dead, lying in a box six feet underground...

TRAVIS
Death is like the time before you were born. You're nothing, you don't exist...

RICHARD
...While life goes on without me. Think of all the great stuff I'll miss.

TRAVIS
But at least before you're born, you're not aware of the fact you don't exist...

RICHARD
I just want to be here to see how things turn out.

TRAVIS
...When you're dying, you know exactly what's coming.

RICHARD
I'm less afraid of dying than I am of being nothing.

TRAVIS
You're teetering on the brink of nothingness, Dave!

RICHARD
I want the future to remember me.

TRAVIS
The future's not what it used to be.

RICHARD
I want to be able to prove I existed.

TRAVIS
I've seen the future and it's a lot like the present, only much, much longer.

RICHARD
I want my own slice of immortality.

TRAVIS
What's the point of immortality if you're just going to spend it all being miserable?

RICHARD
But there has to be more to life than death.

TRAVIS
Life is just a game. And it doesn't matter whether you win or lose, because you are definitely going to lose.

> RICHARD
> ...I can't just disappear!

> TRAVIS
> I understand that, Dave. If all your thoughts and feelings and memories—everything that defines you as a person—is simply going to disappear someday, then what's the point of living, right? Life is a constant struggle against the oblivion of time. Always remember, Dave: You are unique. Just like everyone else.

Travis fades back into the darkness—but not before grabbing a handful of popcorn from a bowl on the floor—and Richard is again watching television.

INT. RICHARD'S APARTMENT - NIGHT

Richard hangs his latest rejection slip, then gazes up at the veil of rejection nearly covering an entire wall of his apartment.

> RICHARD (V.O.)
> That's the third one this week. I am widely unpublished. My works have not appeared in many of the top magazines.... God, who am I trying to kid? I'll never be a writer. I can't even swallow pills without choking. There's a million things I can't do. I can't hit a curveball...

CUT TO: Richard standing in his apartment with a bat. He swings at an imaginary baseball and misses.

> RICHARD (V.O.) (cont.)
> ...I can't hit a fastball...

Again he swings and misses.

> RICHARD (V.O.) (cont.)
> ...I can't hit a ball, period. Never could.

He swings again. Strike three.

> RICHARD (V.O.) (cont.)
> I can't do that thing people do with their tongues...

CUT TO: Richard sticking out his tongue and trying to curl it up into a tube.

> RICHARD (V.O.) (cont.)
> Everyone can do that except me. I can't ski. I swim like a rock. I can't make an F chord on the guitar. I once tried to teach myself how to play. I had this idyllic vision of myself entertaining a small group of friends...

CUT TO: Richard sitting on the floor of his apartment, wearing an avant-garde beard and glasses, strumming expertly on a guitar and singing.

> RICHARD (V.O.) (cont.)
> But then you find out about all these stupid chords you have to learn...

CUT TO: Richard, back to normal, sitting on the floor with a guitar, struggling to bend his fingers into the proper positions.

> RICHARD (V.O.) (cont.)
> ...It's hopeless. I can never approach a set of double doors without picking the one that's locked. I can't even throw a Frisbee...

EXT. A CITY SIDEWALK - DAY

In SLOW MOTION, Richard walks down the sidewalk. A Frisbee sails out of a park and skids to a stop at his feet.

> RICHARD (V.O.)
> I have this recurring nightmare that I'm walking down the sidewalk and a Frisbee lands at my feet and they ask me to throw it back...

Nervously Richard glances around, as a group of KIDS across a field shout for him to toss it back. He picks it up and tries to sail it back to them, but instead it wobbles over on its side, hits the ground, and rolls away. The kids all stare at him with juvenile contempt.

> RICHARD (V.O.) (cont.)
> ...But it just flops over like a wounded duck.... So I bought myself a Frisbee and now I practice alone at night.

INT. RICHARD'S APARTMENT - NIGHT

Alone in his apartment, Richard flutters a Frisbee back and forth across the room.

> RICHARD (V.O.)
> In my own defense, however, I must admit there is one skill I do possess: I have the uncanny ability to shake exactly two aspirin out of a bottle on the first try.

CUT TO: Richard in his bathroom. He opens a bottle of aspirin, shakes two pills into his palm, and looks up at the mirror.

                    RICHARD
        Still got it.

He pops the aspirin into his mouth, tosses back a glass of water, and collapses in a fit of choking.

INT. A LAUNDROMAT - DAY

Richard stands before a pair of washing machines, separating his clothes into colors and whites with expert efficiency.

                    RICHARD (V.O.)
        The last thing I ever wanted was a nice,
        safe, comfortable job. As soon as I get com-
        fortable, I feel death closing in. I have to
        keep moving. I want to be free.... But I
        don't want to end up a corpse crouched in
        a doorway either. And freedom requires
        money.

Richard pulls out a striped shirt and suddenly stops. He stares at it, paralyzed, unable to decide which washer it goes in.

                    RICHARD (V.O.) (cont.)
        Life is full of disappointments. And I am
        full of life.

INT. AN ELEVATOR - DAY

Richard stands alone in the elevator of his apartment building.

CUT TO: Richard imagines himself a baseball player in center field. At the CRACK of the bat, he drifts back to the rear wall of the elevator in SLOW MOTION.

                    SPORTSCASTER (O.S.)
            It's a long fly ball to deep center field.
            Freeman is back, he's at the wall, he leaps...

The CROWD ROARS as Richard leaps and catches the imaginary baseball, then fires it into second base.

                    SPORTSCASTER (O.S.) (cont.)
            He got it! Holy cow! What an amazing
            catch by Freeman!

CUT TO: Richard pointing defiantly at some imaginary foe.

                    RICHARD
            You better watch it, pal.... That's right—you
            better watch your step!

CUT TO: Richard as Norman Bates, in BLACK & WHITE, slicing an imaginary shower curtain to the SCREECH of VIOLINS and the SCREAMS of Janet Leigh.

CUT TO: Richard as Janet Leigh, in BLACK & WHITE, cringing in the corner of the elevator and SCREAMING.

CUT TO: Richard as a mechanical toy soldier, marching stiff-legged and bouncing off the walls of the elevator.

CUT TO: Richard as Travis Bickle.

                    RICHARD
            You talking to me?... Are *you* talking to *me*?

CUT TO: Richard as a heavy-metal rock star. He drops to his knees for a blazing GUITAR SOLO.

CUT TO: Richard peals off a latex mask to reveal a hideous creature beneath.

CUT TO: Richard as the captain of the Starship Enterprise. He crashes back and forth between the walls of the elevator as the ship is rocked by PHASER EXPLOSIONS.

> SCOTTY (O.S.)
> Captain, the engines can't take much more of this!

CUT TO: Richard as a mechanical toy soldier again.

CUT TO: Richard as himself. He smoothes his hair, adjusts his clothes, and quickly resumes a blank expression as the elevator slows to a stop. The door opens and a WOMAN steps on.

> RICHARD (V.O.)
> I've read that some women lift their skirts over their heads when they're alone in an elevator.

At the next floor, several more PEOPLE climb aboard, crowding Richard against the wall.

> RICHARD (V.O.) (cont.)
> Stare straight ahead, don't fidget, don't breathe. Just try to act natural.... Whenever the elevator starts getting crowded, I feel an uncontrollable urge to add up the weights of everyone on board.

Richard glances at each of the passengers, silently estimating their weights, then looks at a sign on the wall that reads: CAPACITY 2,000 LBS. He breathes a sigh of relief—until the door opens again to reveal a hugely OVERWEIGHT WOMAN waiting to board and his eyes widen in terror.

EXT. A CITY SIDEWALK - DAY

A glossy, promotional, 1950s-style documentary trumpets the achievements of hardworking white people, as an army of identical suits and dresses bustles along a big-city sidewalk.

> NARRATOR (V.O.)
> Today's young people are making it big as never before. In an age of unprecedented opportunity, they're on the fast track to wealth and success. All it takes is a little hustle and the proper can-do attitude.

EXT. AN OFFICE BUILDING - DAY

Dressed in an ill-fitting suit and tie, Richard strides to the entrance of a looming glass-and-steel edifice. One by one, he pulls on a series of identical doors, but each of them is locked. Puzzled, he steps back, as the first door swings open from within and a suited MAN steps out. Relieved, Richard heads for the unlocked door, which closes before he can get there and locks. As he struggles with it, another door opens from within and a MAN strides through; Richard rushes over but the same thing happens. It's like he's trapped in a life-size shell game. As he yanks on this door, the first door opens from within again and a WOMAN breezes through. Richard sprints over and slides his body through the narrow opening just before it closes.

INT. THE RECEPTION AREA OF A PRESTIGIOUS FIRM - DAY

His knee bouncing uncontrollably, his hand impulsively smoothing his hair, Richard sits fidgeting on a sofa.

> RICHARD (V.O.)
> God, I hate wearing suits. I always feel like

an imposter, like some guy with a badge is gonna tap on my shoulder and ask if I have a permit to wear this.... Just relax. Project positive body language. Remember to make eye contact. Convey a can-do attitude....

> RECEPTIONIST (O.S.)
> Mr. Freeman?

Richard looks up, startled.

INT. AN OFFICE - DAY

Richard is led into a plush office by a tall, stern, middle-aged man, INTERVIEWER #1, who takes his place between two other men, INTERVIEWERS #2 and #3, each smiling like sharks and seated behind a table.

> INTERVIEWER #1
> Won't you please have a seat?

Richard sits in a small chair opposite them, like a prisoner at a parole hearing.

> INTERVIEWER #1 (cont.)
> We've carefully examined your...

> INTERVIEWER #2
> ...resume and we'd like to ask you a few...

> INTERVIEWER #3
> ...questions. If you don't mind.

Richard swallows uneasily.

> RICHARD
> Shoot.

INTERVIEWERS #1,2,3
(*rapid-fire and overlapping*)
Tell us about yourself. What do you know about our company? Why do you want to work here? What can you do for us that someone else can't? How long would you stay with us? What are you looking for? How would you evaluate your present employer?

INTERVIEWERS (cont.)
(*overlapping*)
Why haven't you found a job before now? Why are you leaving your present position? What is your greatest weakness?

INTERVIEWERS (cont.)
(*overlapping*)
What do you think of our benefits package? How would you describe the essence of success? Where do you want to be in five years? How does this job fit into your plans?

RICHARD
(*overlapping the Interviewers; flustered, trying to keep up*)
I'm, uh— I admire your, uh— I wish to be part of a team effort and help solve a company goal—uh, *problem*, a company prob— What? As long as the relationship is mutual— A position that better ulitizes— ulitizes— ulitizes my—uh, excellent firm that afforded me—

RICHARD (V.O.)
(*overlapping*)
—bunch of sniveling weasels—

RICHARD
—haven't found the right—my ability—I'm something of a—

RICHARD (V.O.)
(*overlapping*)
—obsessive-compulsive—

RICHARD
—perfectionist—

RICHARD (cont.)
—I haven't had a chance—uh, that wasn't—wait, I think—uh, concrete step toward building a foundation on which to build my future earning—

INTERVIEWERS (cont.)
(*overlapping*)
How would you fit into our organization? What are your personal goals at this time? We're looking for someone who knows what he wants—a problem solver—a sense of identity...

RICHARD (V.O.)
(*overlapping*)
I have no idea what I'm saying.

RICHARD
—flexibility is key to any grow— I consider myself a problem solver—strong companies need strong employees—

RICHARD (V.O.)
(*overlapping*)
—stitch in time saves—people in glass houses shouldn't throw—square of the hypotenuse is equal to the sum of the squares of the other two sides.

INTERVIEWER #1
Would you mind singing us your favorite song?

RICHARD
Um... what?

INTERVIEWER #2
Sing.

INTERVIEWER #3
Just sing.

Hesitantly, Richard begins to sing, falteringly and off-key.

RICHARD
(*singing*)
This land is your land/This land is my land/From California/To—

Richard is sweating profusely. The interviewers smile and pat their hands to the music before resuming the rabid inquisition. The voice in Richard's head begins humming the battle theme from *Star Wars*. He can't figure out what to do with his hands.

INTERVIEWERS #1,2,3
(overlapping)
What's the square root of 472? What's the capital of North Dakota? How many fingers am I holding up? Is that supposed to be a joke? I got your nose! Who do you think I am, your mother? Money doesn't grow on trees, you know. Does anybody really know what time it is? Does anybody really care? Look at me when I'm talking to you!

RICHARD
(overlapping the Interviewers)
I can start as soon as— Yes, I'm confident that my—what? No, I— Uh...

RICHARD (V.O.)
(overlapping)
Oh, God. I don't know what to do with my hands. They're like these alien things attached to my arms....

INTERVIEWER #1
How do you react to criticism?

RICHARD
I believe it.

INTERVIEWER #1
What is the first word that pops into your head when I say...

INTERVIEWERS #1,2,3
(simultaneously)
...Richard Freeman?

Suddenly the room is deathly silent. The only sound is the TICKING of a clock—or is it Richard's heart? The interviewers stare at him eagerly as he struggles to come up with an answer.

> RICHARD (V.O.)
> Failure. Fraud. Imposter. No, come on, think, think...

> INTERVIEWER #1
> Do you have any questions for us?

> RICHARD (V.O.)
> *(rapidly, fading to silence)*
> Why is this position open? How would you like the job done better? What are your long-term objectives? Where are the opportunities for advancement?...

> RICHARD
> Uh... can I go now?

INT. A FAST-FOOD RESTAURANT - DAY

Richard stands behind the counter in a silly uniform, paper hat, and wireless headset.

> RICHARD
> Welcome to Burger Barn. Can I take your order, please?

He repeats an order into the mic, wincing at a SQUEAL OF FEEDBACK and gazing out at CUSTOMERS glumly picking at their Chicken McByproducts beneath a giant picture of the company's clown mascot.

> RICHARD (cont.)
> Boffo Burger... Boffo Burger... Double

Cheese Boffo... Barnyard Salad... Bushel o' Fries...

> RICHARD (V.O.)
> (*overlapping*)
> That has got to be the unfunniest clown in the world. I mean, he's a clown, right? But has he ever done anything funny? Has he ever made anyone laugh?... All over the world, millions of people eat the same food with the same taste every single day. No fun, no surprises. Even the clown can't make them laugh.

INT. RICHARD'S APARTMENT - NIGHT

Richard sits in front of the TV.

> RICHARD (V.O.)
> One Saturday afternoon when I was six years old, my father took me to see Bozo the Clown in person. Bozo did a little magic show and invited my father up on stage to play a kind of shell game....

INT. A SHOPPING MALL - DAY

A CROWD of LAUGHING CHILDREN and their PARENTS surrounds a small stage where BOZO THE CLOWN is leading several children and RICHARD'S FATHER to a table. A SIX-YEAR-OLD RICHARD watches with pride and trepidation.

> RICHARD (V.O.)
> Bozo would shuffle three coconut shells and ask my father to pick the one with a hidden Ping-Pong ball. But no matter how

hard he tried, my father could never pick the right shell.

Again and again, Bozo lifts the empty shell that Richard's father has chosen, and the children scream with laughter.

> RICHARD (V.O.) (cont.)
> Somehow Bozo made that ball jump from shell to shell as if by magic, and each time the kids would laugh louder and louder, until they were nearly screaming with laughter, and my father's face turned red.

Richard's father comes down from the stage to the children's jeers, takes his son by the hand without saying a word, and leads him from the crowd.

INT. YOUNG RICHARD'S BEDROOM - NIGHT

Six-year-old Richard lies under the covers, listening intently to SCRAPING SOUNDS coming from the kitchen downstairs.

> RICHARD (V.O.)
> As I lay awake in bed that night, I could hear him downstairs at the kitchen table, trying to figure out how Bozo had done it...

INT. THE KITCHEN OF RICHARD'S PARENTS' HOUSE - NIGHT

Hunched over the table, Richard's father slides three overturned bowls around as if it were a matter of life and death.

> RICHARD (V.O.)
> ...How Bozo the Clown had humiliated

him in front of all those kids. For hours on end. But it was hopeless, and finally he gave up and went to bed.

INT. YOUNG RICHARD'S BEDROOM - NIGHT

Lying in bed, Richard listens to the sound of his father's FOOTSTEPS mounting the stairs.

> RICHARD (V.O.)
> My father was never the same after that. He had been the kind of man who never thought very deeply about things, blessed with the faith that God was in heaven and all was right with the universe. But now his view of the world was shattered....

INT. RICHARD'S PARENTS' BEDROOM - NIGHT

Richard's father glumly undresses for bed, ignoring the unheard harangue of his wife, RICHARD'S MOTHER, behind him. Slowly his figure fades into darkness.

> RICHARD (V.O.)
> ...It was 1968, and nothing ever made sense again. Vietnam, Watergate, Richard Nixon... How could things ever make sense when we lived in a world of cosmic absurdity where a clown, a kiddie-show clown, could subvert the physical laws of the universe?... My father never did figure out the secret of Bozo's shell game. And ten years later he died, a bitter shell of a man. And for the rest of my life I've had the feeling that... Bozo the Clown killed my father.

INT. RICHARD'S APARTMENT - NIGHT

Richard stands before a mirror, dressed as a clown.

INT. RICHARD'S APARTMENT - NIGHT

Richard sits in front of the TV, zapping through channels with the remote, mesmerized by each passing image—two tiny pictures reflected in his eyes.

> RICHARD (V.O.)
> Television is the next best thing to talking to yourself.

> VOICES FROM THE TV (O.S.)
> ...Next the Eskimos remove the seal's internal organs— Go ahead, make my day— This week we'll be discussing problems with your converter box— Folger's café es muy delicioso!— Put your hands on the TV screen now, my friends, and feel the divine healing power of video— Let's have a warm welcome for Mr. Tony Randall!...

Richard stops to applaud along with the TV audience.

> RICHARD (V.O.)
> *(overlapping)*
> Television has defined my life.... When I was young, I yearned to believe that someplace there was a town where the Brady kids and the Partridge kids and the Douglas kids went to school together. Where Lucy and Ricky and Rob and Laura lived in houses side by side. Where all of life's problems could be solved in half an hour.

>   And where, every Saturday, Wile E. Coyote
>   died for your sins.
>
>   VOICES FROM THE TV (O.S.) (cont.)
>   ...Leading economic indicators are down
>   for the third— In Bali, Michael Caine and
>   his lovely wife Shakira— Over the past three
>   centuries, there have been more than 200
>   reported cases of spontaneous human
>   combustion....
>
>   RICHARD (V.O.)
>   I am the end result of everything I've seen
>   on TV.

EXT. A CITY STREET - DAY

Seated behind the wheel of his rented Ford, Richard is again stuck in traffic. The clock on the dashboard reads 11:25. HORNS are HONKING and tempers are beginning to flare.

>   RICHARD (V.O.)
>   Always walk fast. Never look a panhandler
>   in the pan. Act crazy and the muggers will
>   leave you alone. Ignore all questions from
>   strangers. To speak or be spoken to is a
>   threatening act.

Richard's gaze wanders along a busy sidewalk and the spectrum of humanity before him: A TEENAGER carrying a radio the size of a New York studio apartment. A MUSLIM ON ROLLER SKATES selling incense. An ANGRY MAN stomping down the sidewalk and yelling, "I'll kill her! I'll kill her!" An earnest YOUNG MAN aggressively stuffing flyers into everyone's hands or pockets. A STREET-CORNER PREACHER loudly chastising "Fornicators!" A MAN and his dog, both wearing gas masks. A LONELY OLD LADY walking her dog, each of them limping, each of them dull and glassy-eyed, each of them wearing a threadbare sweater.

> RICHARD (V.O.) (cont.)
> People were not meant to live like this, caged together like animals in a zoo. It makes them neurotic, violent.... Eight million of us on this one tiny island. It gives the city such an oppressive weight. Every day I'm afraid the whole thing is going to sink into the sea.

INT. A CITY BUS - DAY

Richard stares across the aisle at his reflection in the window, appearing and disappearing like a ghost against the storefronts displaying sullen, seductive mannequins.

> RICHARD (V.O.)
> My mother was a clinging, manipulative woman. My father, earnest and simpleminded. His primary job in the house was to keep the peace between my mother and all the people who got on her nerves....

INT. THE KITCHEN OF RICHARD'S PARENTS' HOUSE - DAY

Six-year-old Richard sits at the table, quietly eating his breakfast cereal and glancing fretfully between his parents. His father's face is buried in a newspaper, while his mother restlessly puffs on a cigarette. The tension between them is like a burning fuse.

> RICHARD (V.O.)
> ...My job was to be happy and normal. My

father's single act of rebellion was an affair he had with our neighbor. My mother knew all about it, of course—nothing like that could get by her—but she desperately needed the stability he gave her, and so for twenty years she kept quiet.

INT. RICHARD'S PARENTS' BEDROOM - DAY

Richard's father sits on the edge of the bed in his shorts, putting on two mismatched socks.

> RICHARD (V.O.)
> For twenty years she laid out his clothes on the bed every morning before he went to work: a gray flannel suit, a black tie, a white shirt, and two socks, one red and one green.... My father was color-blind, and he never caught on.

EXT. RICHARD'S PARENTS' HOUSE - DAY

On a gray winter day, Richard's mother, dressed in mourning, stands on the sidewalk outside her front door in the snow, holding an urn.

> RICHARD (V.O.)
> When he died in the winter of '78, my mother had his body cremated and sprinkled his ashes on the sidewalk in front of our house, to melt the snow.

She tips over the urn and sprinkles black ashes into the snow.

> RICHARD (V.O.) (cont.)
> She said, "I always knew someday he'd make himself useful."

INT. RICHARD'S MOTHER'S CONDO - DAY

Richard sits morosely on a pristine white sofa in his mother's immaculately overstuffed living room, thoughtlessly thumbing through a fashion magazine.

> MOTHER (O.S.)
> David? Where are you?

Richard says nothing as his mother, 50, struts into the room, her face the overwrought creation of some demented beautician.

> MOTHER
> Oh, there you are. Why didn't you answer? It's so dark in here, how can you see? Don't you want the light on?

> RICHARD
> No, that's okay, I—

Without waiting for him to answer, she flicks on the light.

> MOTHER
> There, isn't that better?

> RICHARD
> Thanks.

With a sigh, she sits down in a chair with a shameless middle-class self-assurance and lights a cigarette.

> RICHARD (V.O.)
> Her house always smells like nail polish and cigarettes.

MOTHER
So... Are you still sleeping on the floor?

RICHARD
(*with resigned annoyance*)
Yes.

MOTHER
Honestly, David, I don't know how you can live like that. Why don't you buy a bed?

RICHARD
I have a mattress.

MOTHER
You can't live like a savage forever. Now what are you going to do about furniture? Do they have stores where you live? Do you need money? If you need money, I'm sure your Uncle Phil would let you borrow—

RICHARD
No, I don't need money.

MOTHER
Maybe if you got a better job, you could afford to buy a bed.

Richard, annoyed, doesn't say anything.

MOTHER (cont.)
Hmm? Don't you think? David?

RICHARD
I said I— I like the job I have.

MOTHER
You like it? Really? Working in that restaurant? I can't imagine there's much money in that. Is there? Or are you just saying that? Hmm? David?
(pause)
Why don't you ask Uncle Phil if he has any nice jobs for you. I'm sure he wouldn't mind—

RICHARD
No.

MOTHER
No? Did you say no? Why not?

RICHARD
Because... I can find my own job. I don't need his help.

MOTHER
Really? Have you been looking? I thought you said you like the job you have now?

RICHARD (V.O.)
Damn. I have to be more careful.

MOTHER
David? Didn't you just say that?

RICHARD
I've been thinking about getting a new job, okay?

MOTHER
Then I guess you don't like your job after

all, if you're looking for a new one. Right?
(pause)
David? Isn't that right?

RICHARD
(giving up)
Yes.

MOTHER
What kind of job are you looking for?

RICHARD
I don't know. Maybe something in publishing.

MOTHER
Publishing? Is there good money in that?

RICHARD
No, there's no money in that.

MOTHER
Why don't you take some computer courses? That's where the big money is these days. Let me show you that article—I cut it out for you....

She starts to get up.

RICHARD
No, I don't want to take computer courses. I hate computers.

MOTHER
Well, you know, David, you can't always do what you want in life. You'll have to learn that someday. Don't you think? Hmm?

> RICHARD (V.O.)
> Just agree with whatever she says.

> MOTHER
> You're not getting any younger. I don't see why you don't ask Phil for a job. He *is* your uncle. Do you want me to give you his number?

> RICHARD
> No, you don't have to—

> MOTHER
> I bet you don't even have his number. Let me just get a pencil....

She gets up and goes to the kitchen, writes down the number on a slip of paper, and returns to the living room.

> MOTHER (cont.)
> I'm sure he'll be happy to hear from you. That company of his must have hundreds of jobs.

Richard sighs in resignation.

> MOTHER (cont.)
> What's wrong?

> RICHARD
> What? Nothing.

> MOTHER
> You sighed.

> RICHARD
> No, I didn't.

MOTHER
Yes, you did. I heard you.

RICHARD
I did not.

MOTHER
What's wrong?

RICHARD
Nothing.

MOTHER
Then why did you sigh?

RICHARD
I didn't sigh.

MOTHER
You don't want to call him?

RICHARD
I'll call him.

MOTHER
Do you want me to call him for you?

RICHARD
I said I'd call him.

He takes the paper and stuffs it in his pocket, while his mother returns to the kitchen.

MOTHER
I know you won't call him. I'll talk to him tomorrow.

She opens the back door to let in her miniature dog, Muffin.

> MOTHER (cont.)
> (*in a high-pitched baby voice*)
> And who's this? Who is this little lady? Does mummy's little Muffin want to come in now? Do you? Do you?

She picks up the dog and carries it into the living room.

> MOTHER (cont.)
> Who's that? Who's that? That's your big brother! Yes, it is. Go say hi. Go say hi now. Hi, big brother!

She releases the dog. It YAPS excitedly, jumps onto the couch where Richard is sitting, and licks his face. Richard cringes and turns away.

> MOTHER (cont.)
> (*in her normal voice*)
> Oh, David, let her lick you. That's just her way of saying I love you.

The dog jumps down and runs back to mummy sitting in her chair.

> MOTHER (cont.)
> (*in a high-pitched baby voice*)
> Isn't it? I wuv you! I wuv you, big brother! Is Muffin hungry? Is poor little Muffy starving? Does Muffy want her din-din? Do you? Do you want your din-din?

> RICHARD (V.O.)
> My God. If she had treated me half as well

> as she treats that dog, I might have had a
> happy childhood.

Suddenly the dog growls, bares its fangs, and lunges at mummy's neck, sinking its teeth into her powdered white flesh. The woman gasps and falls to the floor.

> MOTHER
> Oh, Muffin! No! No! Bad dog! Oh, David, help!

Like a demon, the dog tears at her throat, fountains of blood soiling the perfect white carpet. The almost imperceptible hint of a smile flashes across Richard's face as he stares at the pale, prostrate form and the little dog happily lapping up blood.

> MOTHER (O.S.)
> (from the kitchen)
> David, would you help me set the table? I
> hope these vegetables didn't overcook....

The spell is broken and Richard gets up.

INT. RICHARD'S MOTHER'S CONDO - NIGHT

Richard sits at the dining room table while his mother serves dinner with a cigarette in her mouth. He stares at the ash dangling dangerously over his plate.

> MOTHER
> Do you remember Steve Feldman?

> RICHARD
> No.

> MOTHER
> Yes, you do. He married Shirley's second

cousin, the one who stuttered, the one from Pittsburgh? You remember, don't you?

RICHARD
(lying)
Oh, yeah, right, Steve Feldman.

MOTHER
Well, he just had a massive heart attack. Forty-two years old. Can you believe that? Shirley said his arteries were like peanut butter, that's how clogged he was. Just like that and he was gone. Isn't that amazing? David? I said, isn't that amazing—

Richard doesn't respond. He's watching his mother ladle thick globs of artery-clogging sauce over his vegetables.

MOTHER (cont.)
You look so thin. Have you been eating?

RICHARD (V.O.)
Oh, my God—I forgot to eat!

Richard tries to take the plate from her hand, but she continues ladling.

RICHARD
That's enough, thanks—

MOTHER
What? You used to love my special sauce when you were little. You'd put it on anything...

RICHARD
Really, that's—

                    MOTHER
...vegetables, chips, pretzels—you name it. "Any more special sauce?" you'd ask. You probably don't remember. You used to be so cute.

                    RICHARD (V.O.)
Forget it, it's hopeless.

                    MOTHER
What was that?

                    RICHARD
                    (startled)
Nothing.

CUT TO: Richard and his mother eating dinner.

                    MOTHER
So... Are you still trying to be a writer?

                    RICHARD
Yes.

                    MOTHER
What kind of things do you write about?

He starts to answer but she cuts him off.

                    MOTHER (cont.)
I know! Why don't you write a story about your cousin Mark?

Richard just stares at her.

                    MOTHER (cont.)
You know, the one who lost his arm in that

boating accident and became a banker?
He's *very* successful.
>(pause)

That would be an interesting story, don't
you think? David? Hmm?

CUT TO: Richard and his mother, still sitting at the table.

> MOTHER
> ...I think you spend too much time alone.
> You should get out more, meet people. Do
> you have a girlfriend? Whatever happened
> to that Kathy girl? She was nice. Don't
> make that face. What's wrong? Don't you
> like girls? Don't you even *want* a girlfriend?

CUT TO: Richard and his mother sitting in the living room.

> MOTHER
> (after a long awkward silence)
> So... Do you like your hair that way?

Richard throws his head back in exasperation.

> RICHARD (V.O.)
> Oh God, just open up a vein, why don't
> you?

> MOTHER
> I'm just asking. I don't see what you get so
> upset about. The styles change, you know.
> Maybe that's why you don't have a girl-
> friend. Did you ever think of that? David?
> Did you ever think of that? Hmm?

Her voice fades into silence.

INT. A CAREER PLANNING CENTER - DAY

Leafing through brochures, Richard watches a TV monitor showing a bland, earnest, clean-cut YOUNG MAN talking about his career.

> YOUNG MAN (on TV)
> I'm not just a student. I'm also a businessman, an entrepreneur. Employers look at my resume and see that I've dealt with real-life situations. Leading my very own management team and interfacing with the nation's top CEOs has enabled me to prioritize my classroom functions....

> RICHARD (V.O.)
> *(overlapping)*
> God, this is so depressing. My resume has so many dead-end jobs it's starting to look like a rap sheet.... Look at this guy. He looks like one of the pod people from *Invasion of the Body Snatchers*. His whole future is planned down to the last detail. There has to be more to life than that.

INT. A CONVENIENCE STORE - DAY

Richard stands in a long line at the lottery counter, behind a sullen FAT WOMAN in curlers, who barks her order.

> FAT WOMAN
> Gimme 7, 9, 16 on 3 times 12; 4, 19, 21, and 30 on 7 times 10; plus four dozen Quik Piks, two dozen Lottos, and—

RICHARD (V.O.)
While millions of Japanese toil sixteen hours a day at the Sony factory, we earn our money the old-fashioned way: lottery tickets.

INT. RICHARD'S APARTMENT - NIGHT

Sitting on the floor in front of the TV, Richard scratches off the little squares on his ticket.

CUT TO: Richard standing in the center of his apartment, surrounded by the POP and flash of cameras, holding up a giant cardboard check and wearing a blank expression.

REPORTER (O.S.)
What are you going to do with the money?

RICHARD
I plan on using the money to finance a revolution to overthrow the government of the United States.

CUT TO: Reality. Richard stares in dismay at his ticket.

RICHARD
Damn.

RICHARD (V.O.)
Lotteries are like a tax on the stupid.

INT. RICHARD'S APARTMENT - NIGHT

Sitting in front of the TV, Richard gazes at the ceiling, trying to identify the BANGING, SCRAPING, POUNDING NOISES coming from upstairs. He clenches his jaw in annoyance.

> RICHARD (V.O.)
> I'm convinced the guy who lives above me has opened a bowling alley.

Richard's eyes track an imaginary ball as it RUMBLES across the floor and CRASHES into the pins. With a broom handle, he raps on the ceiling. The NOISES stop momentarily, then continue as before. He raps again, harder, but it has no effect. Frustrated, Richard goes back to the TV. He turns up the volume and covers his ears, but his eyes drift back to the ceiling.

CUT TO: Richard lying awake in bed, as RAUCOUS MUSIC from a party upstairs literally vibrates his mattress. He picks up the phone and dials. The MUSIC stops and he watches the ceiling, as FOOTSTEPS cross the upstairs floor.

> NEIGHBOR (on phone)
> Hello?

Richard is about to say something, then freezes and quickly hangs up. He stares at the ceiling and waits for the MUSIC to resume, then grabs his jacket and bolts out the door.

INT. A MOVIE THEATER - NIGHT

Amid perfect silence, Richard sits by himself in a nearly empty theater, eating Milk Duds one after another.

> RICHARD (V.O.)
> An empty theater is like seeing the world before it began. It's always been my refuge.... You know how people claim to remember exactly where they were when Kennedy was shot? Well, what I remember is where I was the first time I saw John

> Nance stab the mutant baby monster in *Eraserhead*.

The lights come down and the movie projector CLATTERS to life.

> RICHARD (V.O.) (cont.)
> Alone, in the dark, surrounded by strangers, you're at your most vulnerable. That guy behind you, he could be a killer, for all you know.... But the stars on the screen have no bodies; they can never die. They're nothing but spirits of shadow and light. In here the burdens of living are lifted and I feel as if I'm one with them.

Slowly Richard floats out of his seat. With his arms outstretched, he drifts like an angel over the heads of the crowd toward the screen.

CUT TO: The annoying CRACKLE of a candy wrapper being opened as slowly as possible by a WOMAN sitting behind him jolts Richard back to reality. The noise seems to go on forever. Impulsively, he turns around, grabs the candy out of her hand, rips off the wrapper, and shoves it back at her.

CUT TO: Reality. Richard silently seethes until the woman is finished.

INT. A MOVIE THEATER - NIGHT

YOUNG RICHARD, about three, watches a movie with his parents.

> RICHARD (V.O.)
> When I was a kid, I used to wonder where

the characters on the screen went after the
movie was over.

As young Richard and his parents walk up the aisle with the rest of the audience, he stares over his shoulder. Suddenly he scampers away, back down the aisle toward the screen. Reaching up on his toes, he pulls aside the curtain and tries to discover what's hidden behind.

> RICHARD (V.O.) (cont.)
> I used to imagine they lived back there, in a secret room. Ghostly actors laughing and sharing drinks after the show.

Behind the screen, young Richard catches a glimpse of translucent ACTORS congratulating one another on a good show. His eyes widen to behold this forbidden wonder, but a hairy adult hand suddenly yanks the curtain back into place. Richard looks up to see a grim USHER, slapping a flashlight into his palm. He scampers away to his parents, but his eyes still linger on the magical screen.

INT. A MOVIE THEATER - NIGHT

Richard again is peeking behind the theater's velvet curtain, but this time he's a grown-up and wearing an usher's uniform. He's startled by the booming voice of the MANAGER from the back of the theater.

> MANAGER
> Freeman, what the hell are you doing? I thought I told you to tear tickets. Come on, move it!

Richard picks up his bucket and mop and hurries up the aisle.

INT. RICHARD'S APARTMENT - NIGHT

In the dead of night, while a sheaf of pages sits on the floor, Richard obsessively cleans. He still has no furniture and the room is spotless, so he scrubs invisible specks from the floor, chips away at a defrosting freezer, combs the bristles of his toothbrush—anything to avoid those blank, beckoning pages.

> RICHARD (V.O.)
> Sometimes these blank sheets haunt me like ghosts. Sometimes the beat of my own heart will be so distracting I can't write a word. Other times I'll find any excuse not to write. But mostly I clean. Cleaning becomes the sole focus of my life. But in the end it's all futile, isn't it? We live in a chaotic, unpredictable universe. Cosmic forces beyond our control twist and shred vast reaches of space and matter. And no matter how many times I scrub the floor of my bathroom, it's still just one piece of a random universe. There's no cleanser in the world that can change that.

INT. RICHARD'S APARTMENT - NIGHT

In darkness Richard lies on his mattress, shifting, unable to sleep, memorizing the pattern of cracks in his ceiling and listening to the BEAT of his heart.

> RICHARD (V.O.)
> What is it that keeps your heart beating twenty-four hours a day? There's no battery, no cord to plug in—it just seems to go all by itself. So what's to prevent it from stopping

all by itself?... Oh, God. I'm having chest pains. Sometimes at night my heart beats so loud I'm afraid the neighbors are going to complain.

A sudden POUNDING on the wall is followed by an angry voice.

                    VOICE (O.S.)
Hey in there! Stop beating your heart so loud, we're trying to sleep!

                    RICHARD (V.O.)
I wonder if a person can die from insomnia. Countless volumes have been written on sleep deprivation, and I've stayed up late many nights reading them, but it doesn't help. I still can't sleep. Is it the fear that I might not wake up? Or the fear of what I'll see there. The demons that haunt us during the day are suppressed and released at night in our dreams, but what happens to the insomniac's demons? Where do *they* go at night?

CUT TO: Richard watching television at 4 o'clock in the morning. Travis stands by the window, nearly hidden in shadows.

                    TRAVIS
Are you still awake?

                    RICHARD
I've never been more awake.

                    TRAVIS
What are you doing up so late?

RICHARD
Dying.... Little by little, cell by cell—I can't afford to waste any time asleep. I might miss something good on TV.

TRAVIS
From the moment you're born, you're dying.

RICHARD
No, I'm serious. My brain cells—

TRAVIS
Every human being is a terminal patient.

RICHARD
Did you know they're dying at the rate of 50,000 a day? I can almost feel myself getting dumber. I think I have Alzheimer's.

TRAVIS
Dave, your life is like an endless talk show without any guests.

RICHARD
My whole body is decaying—just thinking about it causes me stress. So I *try* to relax, but when I can't, that gets me even more stressed, and then I start thinking about—

TRAVIS
You know, studies have shown that people who don't think about death live longer.

RICHARD
Is that supposed to make me feel better?

TRAVIS
So what's bothering you now? I mean, besides everything on the planet.

RICHARD
This.

Richard hands Travis a thick medical tome.

TRAVIS
The Complete Guide to Symptoms?

RICHARD
The hypochondriac's bible. I never should have bought it—it's giving me a headache.... Headache—quick, look up "headache."

Travis flips to the H's and starts listing headache causes.

TRAVIS
Headache, let's see.... Meningitis. Encephalitis. Subdural hematoma. Brain tumor—

RICHARD
Brain tumor, I knew it.

TRAVIS
Oh, give me a break.

RICHARD
I think my vision is getting blurry...

TRAVIS
Give me a flying bucket of break. I'm sorry you're dying, but everyone has it hard.

                    RICHARD
            ...I'm so tired.

                    TRAVIS
            You're not alive enough to be tired.

                    RICHARD
            Can't you just give me some advice or a pill
            or something?

                    TRAVIS
            I'm not wasting my time with you. Life is
            too short.

Travis fades back into the shadows and Richard is watching an old gangster film on TV.

INT. A BANK - DAY

Richard stands in the lobby. He glances at the bank's security camera. Its grainy, BLACK & WHITE view shows him looking awkward and tentative.

                    RICHARD (V.O.)
            I think the key is to act quickly. Don't
            waste any time. Spend no more than ninety
            seconds inside....

Richard writes on the back of a deposit slip: "This is a stickup. I have a gun. Hand over all of your—" But he runs out of space. He tries to squeeze in the last few letters, then crumples the slip and starts over: "This is a stickup—" He scratches out "stickup" and writes "holdup" beneath it, then crosses out "holdup" and writes "robbery." Then he scratches out "robbery" and tears up the slip. Too sloppy. He starts over.

> RICHARD (V.O.) (cont.)
> Don't bother with the vault—that takes too long. Just stick with the cash drawers. And don't make a scene. Be quick and professional.

Richard stumbles over the velvet rope and gets in line.

> RICHARD (V.O.) (cont.)
> The only thing I'd be worried about is some trigger-happy security guard who wants to play hero.

He glances nervously at the SECURITY GUARD, a glum, balding middle-aged man standing listlessly near a potted plant.

> RICHARD (V.O.) (cont.)
> And who can blame him? The guy must have the most boring job on earth, standing all day in that phony cop outfit, like it's his job to enforce the law of gravity. Add an inferiority complex because he's not a real policeman and he's probably desperate for some action.

Richard leaves the teller's window with a heavy bag of cash, casually walks across the lobby, and sits down in a chair.

> RICHARD (V.O.) (cont.)
> I look at it this way: If I get away with it, I'm rich, I don't have to work anymore, and I can spend all my time writing. If I don't get away with it, I go to prison, I don't have to work anymore, and I can spend all my time writing. Either way I come out ahead.

Two POLICE OFFICERS hurry into the bank with their guns drawn. The BANK MANAGER meekly points out Richard, sitting serenely, and the officers approach him.

> RICHARD
> I thought you guys would never get here.

He gets up and they lead him out the door.

INT. A PRISON - DAY

Two tall, beefy PRISON GUARDS lead Richard, in a prison uniform, down a long gray corridor flanked by cells.

> RICHARD (V.O.)
> Prison wouldn't be so bad, would it? Every writer should spend some time here—it gives you credentials. Free food, free clothing, a warm dry place to sleep at night, and all the free time a man could ever want. My God, it's almost like winning the lottery.

The guards open a cell and shove Richard inside. They lock the door with a CLANG and march back down the corridor, as Richard surveys his new home with satisfaction.

> RICHARD (V.O.) (cont.)
> On the outside you've got bills and rent and mindless work. Now, I ask you, who's really behind bars?

CUT TO: Richard at a desk in his idealized cell, typing his manuscript. He leans back reflectively and puffs on a cigarette, a thick stack of pages neatly piled beside him. On a shelf overhead is an impressive array of books.

                    RICHARD (V.O.) (cont.)
               I'd spend all day working on the Great
               American Novel. No job, no distractions—
               just me, my thoughts, and my Smith-
               Corona. At night I could finally read all
               the great books I've never had time for—
               Proust and Tolstoy and Dostoyevsky....
               God, what a life.

INT. THE VESTIBULE OF AN ATM - DAY

In the bright glass-and-tile space, Richard stands in line behind a LITTLE OLD LADY. On the floor near the door is a HOMELESS MAN.

                    RICHARD (V.O.)
               ...All I need to do now is get myself ar-
               rested and then I can finally relax.

The old lady bends down and speaks directly into the cash slot.

                    OLD LADY
               Hello? I would like to— Hello? Is anybody
               there—?

She taps on the machine and waits for an answer, as Richard stares in frustrated disbelief.

CUT TO: Richard punches the button to withdraw $20. The cash slot opens and the ATM spits out two, not one, crisp $20 bills. He hesitates.

                    RICHARD (V.O.)
               Uh-oh. What do I do now?

Nervously he glances around.

RICHARD (V.O.) (cont.)
               I should really give it back, but... the bank
               is closed. No, what am I saying?

He starts to pocket the money.

               RICHARD (V.O.) (cont.)
               Wait! What if it's a trap? What if there's an
               FBI agent waiting to jump out and grab—

He glances at the homeless man asleep on the floor.

               RICHARD (V.O.) (cont.)
               It's him! I bet it's him! Wow, good dis-
               guise... No, that's ridiculous. It's probably
               just a computer error.

The ATM flashes the message DO YOU WANT ANOTHER TRANS-
ACTION?

               RICHARD (V.O.) (cont.)
               Hey, maybe if I do it again I'll get even
               more!.... No, no, don't press your luck.
               Just take the extra and go. It's their prob-
               lem, not mine.

He quickly hits NO, stuffs the bills into his pocket, and hurries
for the door.

               RICHARD (V.O.) (cont.)
               God, I'm gonna feel guilty about this all
               day, I know it. Maybe I should just find the
               nearest cop and turn myself in.

                    HOMELESS MAN
               Spare a quarter, sir?

Richard hesitates at the door, then impulsively stuffs the $20 bills into the hand of the homeless man and hurries out.

> HOMELESS MAN (cont.)
> Thank you, sir. Thank you very much.

EXT. A CITY SIDEWALK - DAY

Richard walks down the street, consumed in his thoughts.

> RICHARD (V.O.)
> I was born feeling guilty, I can't help it. Like when I hear about some horrific crime on the news. I know I didn't do it, but... what if I did and just don't remember? What if I have a split personality? What—

A car pulls up beside him and the DRIVER shouts through the window.

> DRIVER
> Excuse me!

> RICHARD
> *(startled)*
> What?

> DRIVER
> Could you tell me how to get to the train station?

> RICHARD
> Yeah, just keep going straight until you hit the second light, then take a left and drive for about ten blocks.

> DRIVER
> Okay, thanks.

The car drives away and Richard continues walking.

> RICHARD (V.O.)
> ...What if I'm leading a double life I'm not even aware of? Maybe that's why I'm so tired every morning.

Suddenly he stops.

> RICHARD (V.O.) (cont.)
> Did I say "left"? Oh, crap. I meant "right." Dammit....

He continues walking, faster, glancing over his shoulder.

> RICHARD (V.O.) (cont.)
> Now I have to spend the rest of the day worrying that I'll run into this guy again, like he's gonna be looking for me.

INT. A SUBWAY TRAIN - NIGHT

Late at night, Richard sits on a nearly deserted subway train. He glances anxiously at the other PASSENGERS.

> RICHARD (V.O.)
> It pays to be paranoid when you live in the city. Paranoids live to see another day.... Don't look anyone in the eye—but don't take your eye off of anyone. And don't ever say "please" or "excuse me"—they'll just take it as a sign of weakness. Politeness is like an invitation to be victimized.

The door between cars suddenly CRASHES open and FOUR TEENAGE BOYS, laughing and shouting, bound onto the train and surround Richard. One of them stares at his sneakers.

>   TEENAGE BOY
>   Nice shoes, homes. Looks like my size, too.

The other boys laugh. Richard turns in panic to his fellow passengers, who look away with disinterest. Sweat streams down his neck. He sees his photo beneath a tabloid headline screaming SUBWAY SLAYING!, until the door CRASHES open again, the boys jump out, and Richard breathes a sigh of relief.

>   RICHARD (V.O.)
>   A shadow can fall across anyone. I have to
>   be prepared....

EXT. A CITY STREET - DAY

Behind the wheel of his rented Ford, Richard is again stuck in traffic. The clock on the dashboard reads 11:33. He gazes out the window at the vacant faces of PEOPLE walking by.

>   RICHARD (V.O.)
>   It's a city of extremes, a city of the filthy
>   rich and the filthy. Sometimes I think this
>   place is proof that hell is full and the dead
>   are walking the earth. It's like a slow apoca-
>   lypse. They all look shell-shocked, as if the
>   bomb has already dropped. Day by day the
>   air gets thinner, the sun gets hotter, the
>   gunfire crackles a little bit louder.

INT. RICHARD'S APARTMENT - NIGHT

Richard is lying awake in bed, listening to the RUMBLE of the city at night—the WAIL of SIRENS, the SHOUTS and CRIES and ECHOES of GUNFIRE—and watching the shadows from car headlights chase each other across the ceiling.

> RICHARD (V.O.)
> When you can't sleep, the night seems to go on forever. And the harder you try to get to sleep, the better your hearing gets.... Maybe I'm already asleep and I'm only dreaming I'm awake.

CUT TO: Richard shifting and thrashing in bed, still wide awake.

> RICHARD (V.O.) (cont.)
> The only way to get to sleep is to stop thinking about how I can't get to— Oh, God. I can't take any more of this—I need to lie down. I mean—no, wait. I *am* lying down. I need to get up.

Richard gets up.

INT. A SUPERMARKET - NIGHT

Richard pushes a shopping cart through the bright, nearly deserted aisles of an all-night supermarket.

> RICHARD (V.O.)
> The supermarket at 3 a.m. is like alternate universe. Everything looks normal, but somehow it all seems slightly... surreal.

Richard warily examines his fellow SHOPPERS: a MAN wandering around in pajama bottoms and a scuba mask; a middle-aged WOMAN in a bulletproof pantsuit carrying nothing but Raid! and boxes of Jell-O; a distraught PSYCHOPATH in the cereal aisle.

>   PSYCHOPATH
> Oh, God. They did it again. They rearranged the cereals. They rearranged all the goddamn cereals! Those bastards! Those lousy bastards!

Richard quickly passes by. In the next aisle he finds a MAN holding up two loaves of bread and speaking aloud to no one.

>   MAN
> The day-old bread is cheaper, but I'll have to eat it fast before it gets too hard. But if I buy the fresh bread, by tomorrow it'll be day-old, so unless I eat it all tonight, the extra money will be wasted. It's like a fucking conspiracy.

Richard turns away to find a wheezing WEIRDO standing much too close to him.

>   RICHARD
> Excuse me.

CUT TO: Richard approaches the registers with his cart.

>   RICHARD (V.O.)
> Always ignore the length of the line and go for the smartest-looking cashier. A smart cashier is up to 84 percent faster than a dumb one.

Richard pulls into an empty lane, where a big-haired, gum-chewing CHECKOUT GIRL is listlessly wiping the counter.

> CHECKOUT GIRL #1
> I'm closed!

He pulls into the next lane, where two more CHECKOUT GIRLS are standing—identical triplets in a noisy conversation—while an OLD LADY laboriously fishes for coins in a tiny change purse. She lays them on the counter one at a time with painful deliberation.

> CHECKOUT GIRL #3
> So I says, "If you want to dress like a tramp, Jimmy's gonna treat you like a tramp."

> CHECKOUT GIRLS #1 & 2
> Tina! You didn't!

> CHECKOUT GIRL #3
> I did. Right to her face!

The old lady loses her count, hesitates, and starts again.

> CHECKOUT GIRL #2
> Was she pissed or what?

> CHECKOUT GIRL #3
> Uh-huh. But I don't care. And I don't care if she tells Jimmy neither. Vinnie's gonna fire him anyways for wrecking Angie's truck.

> OLD LADY
> *(softly, embarrassed)*
> I don't have enough.

> CHECKOUT GIRL #1
> Where'd you hear that?

> CHECKOUT GIRL #3
> Angie told me her own self!

> OLD LADY
> I– I don't–

The cashier turns to the old lady in annoyance.

> CHECKOUT GIRL #3
> What's the matter?

> OLD LADY
> –don't have enough money.

The girl heaves a theatrical sigh, then yells across the store.

> CHECKOUT GIRL #3
> Ronnie! I need the key!

Richard flinches at the sudden screech as RONNIE, the assistant manager, sticks his head out the office door.

> RONNIE
> What's your problem?

> CHECKOUT GIRL #3
> I got a void! I need the key!

> RONNIE
> Oh, jeez...

> CHECKOUT GIRL #3
> It's not my fault! She doesn't have enough money!

Ronnie trudges across the floor with a fat set of keys, while the old lady removes items from her bag apologetically.

> RONNIE
> What the hell am I gonna do with you?

> CHECKOUT GIRL #2
> She said it's not her fault!

> OLD LADY
> I'm sorry.... Oh, wait, I forgot–

She reaches into her purse and pulls out a handful of frail, wrinkled coupons. Richard closes his eyes and sighs.

CUT TO: Richard still waiting in line. A WOMAN in curlers with two screaming KIDS pulls in behind him. Richard eyes her in alarm as she grabs a plastic divider and shoves his groceries forward to make room for her own.

> KID #1
> Mom, Spencer took a candy bar!

> KID #2
> Shut up!

> FAT WOMAN
> Put that back!

The two kids wrestle and Richard peeks into the woman's cart.

> RICHARD (V.O.)
> Yuck.

> KID #1
> Quit it!

                    KID #2

    No, you quit it!

                    KID #1

    No, you quit it!

Not paying attention, the woman wheels her cart into Richard's hip and he winces in pain. Ronnie teases the cashier trying to ring up Richard's groceries, messing with her hairdo as she waves a can of corn back and forth across the scanner, the electronic eye BEEPING in protest.

                    RONNIE

    What'd you do to your hair? It smells like a
    fruit salad.

                CHECKOUT GIRL #3

    Ronnie, stop! Look what you made me do—
    now this thing's broke!

Ronnie starts walking back to the office; the checkout girl shouts after him.

                    RONNIE

    You broke it.

                CHECKOUT GIRL #3

    No, you broke it!

                    RONNIE

    No, you broke it!

                CHECKOUT GIRL #3

    No, you broke it!

And on and on. Wrestling with her screaming kids, the woman behind him again nails her cart into Richard's hip, as the cashier begins ringing up his groceries by hand, punching in a seemingly endless string of digits.

> CHECKOUT GIRL #3 (cont.)
> Way to go, ass-wipe! Now I gotta do all these fucking codes.

Richard stares at a tabloid headline: LIBRARIAN BURSTS INTO FLAMES! SPONTANEOUS COMBUSTION LINKED TO ECLIPSE.

EXT. A CITY SIDEWALK - NIGHT

Richard trudges home with his groceries.

> RICHARD (V.O.)
> We're all doomed, every one of us. For millions of years the earth was ruled by dinosaurs, and then in a flash they were gone. The human race has been around for what? A few thousand years? We like to think we'll be here forever, but someday a plague or a comet will hit, and then we'll be fossils too...

INT. RICHARD'S APARTMENT - NIGHT

On his hands and knees with a can of Raid!, Richard closely observes a cockroach scurrying across the floor.

> RICHARD (V.O.)
> These are the real survivors. They're quick, they're smart, they're indestructible. To their eyes we must look like dinosaurs.

Richard sprays the roach with Raid!, then watches it thrash around on the floor, trying to fight off death.

                    RICHARD (V.O.) (cont.)
               They're not much different from us, really.
               Roaches thrash and flail their legs...

One by one the roaches come out and Richard zaps them with Raid!

                    RICHARD (V.O.) (cont.)
               ...while human beings eat health food and
               jog. It's all the same: a desperate struggle to
               stave off the inevitable.

A solitary roach, dazed and poisoned, wanders among the scattered corpses of his brother roaches, like a wounded soldier on a battlefield.

INT. A MAUSOLEUM - NIGHT

Richard stands in a room filled with PEOPLE dressed in black. They're dancing to music he can't hear and whispering intently to one another. They glance at Richard suspiciously as he makes his way across the room, dizzy and confused by the BUZZ of VOICES. Travis appears, escorting a beautiful WOMAN on each arm.

                         TRAVIS
               Dave! Glad you could make it! You've got
               to try the escargot—it is to die...

Travis and the others drift into darkness, and Richard finds himself in a long corridor lined by rows of marble sarcophagi. At the foot of each one is a video screen bearing an image of the deceased. At the end of the corridor is a glass coffin, draped in black.

A narrow gap in the drapery reveals the sallow, decaying head of a corpse inside. Richard approaches the coffin slowly; it seems to retreat down the hallway. A cockroach scurries across the top. As Richard draws nearer, more roaches appear. He gazes through the opening in the drapery, when suddenly a hand appears from inside and flings the black curtain closed.

INT. RICHARD'S APARTMENT - NIGHT

Richard wakes up in a cold sweat. Feeling something crawling under the covers, he kicks them off in a seizure of panic.

INT. RICHARD'S APARTMENT - DAY

Like the plaintive bleat of an electric sheep, Richard's ALARM CLOCK RINGS. A groggy hand reaches out and gropes in vain for a button to silence the awful noise, finally lifting the clock and SMASHING it against the floor until it's quiet. Richard lies on his mattress looking anything but rested.

> RICHARD (V.O.)
> I purposely set the clock 15 minutes fast so I wouldn't be late, but I've already hit the snooze button twice, so that means the time is actually, uh.... Oh God, I shouldn't have to do math this early in the morning.

EXT. RICHARD'S APARTMENT BUILDING - DAY

Richard steps out the front door of his building, as a noisy TRUCK belching black smoke RUMBLES by.

> RICHARD (V.O.)
> Ah, nothing like that first morning gulp of fresh diesel exhaust fumes.

INT. A VIDEO STORE - DAY

Wearing his brand-new Video Shack name tag, Richard is given a tour by the store manager, MR. PEARSON, a short, damp, balding man, compulsively rearranging boxes.

> MR. PEARSON
> ...This here's sci-fi. Here we keep all your alien movies, your space invaders, your time travel, your postapocalyptic nuclear nightmares, nine-foot rodents, giant insects, slime people, toxic mutations, blood-sucking zombies from another dimension—it's all alphabetical. That means *The Monster From Green Hell* goes with the M's and not with the The's. Think you can handle that?

> RICHARD
> Sure.

> MR. PEARSON
> Okay. This here's the kids' section. Here we keep all your Care Bears, your Ninja Turtles, your Smurfs, your Muppets, your—whoa, what the—?

He pounces on a misplaced box and holds it up peevishly to a clerk behind the counter.

> MR. PEARSON (cont.)
> Keith! What is this doing here?

KEITH, a gangly kid with thick glasses, is leaning over the counter, playing with the laser scanner, waving it back and forth across his palm.

> MR. PEARSON (cont.)
> You've got dope-crazed bikers in the kids' tapes, for Christsakes. The whole section's

a mess. Look at this. Three Stooges mixed with Three Little Pigs, Gummi Bears interbreeding with Care Bears—this is horrible!

               KEITH
I'll get right on it.

               MR. PEARSON
Clean this up—I want all these animals separated.

TIM WILSON walks into the store, unshaven, eating a doughnut. He's wearing a studded black leather vest, a cut-off T-shirt, and sunglasses. He's the assistant manager.

               MR. PEARSON (cont.)
Tim, this is Richard. He starts today. Finish the tour for him, will you? I'm too stressed.

He heads into the office, and Tim begins a half-hearted tour.

               TIM
                 (deadpan)
Hi. I'm Tim. Assistant manager. Hard to believe, isn't it?... Here's the job: You hand out boxes. You put boxes on shelves. Got it?

               RICHARD
Got it.

               TIM
Basically, a slow chimp could handle it. If you could find a chimp willing to work for

this kind of money. Let me guess—you're an actor, right?

                    RICHARD
Writer.

                    TIM
Yeah, we get a lot of unemployed artists working here. They crave the mindless routine. The pay sucks, but personal hygiene is optional.

                    RICHARD
How long have you been here?

                    TIM
Too long. Man, if I knew I was gonna spend the rest of my life in retail management, I'd have put a bullet in my head years ago.

Richard is startled by a strangled CRY of frustration coming from the office.

                    TIM (cont.)
Don't worry about him. It's a height thing. You'll find he needs to insult you on a regular basis, but don't take it personal. Just learn to hide your opinions, beliefs, thoughts, feelings, hopes, dreams, ambitions, and you'll be okay.

INT. THE VIDEO STORE - DAY

Richard is kneeling on the floor, pricing a stack of blank videotapes. He checks the clock and sighs with boredom.

                    RICHARD (V.O.)
What am I doing here? I should be—I don't know, networking or something.... Do you ever get the feeling time has slowed to a crawl yet your whole life is whizzing before your eyes?

INT. RICHARD'S APARTMENT - NIGHT

In the dead of night, Richard sits in the dark, his eyes half-closed, with the phone in his hand, listening to a lonely, desperate VOICE on the other end of the line.

                    RICHARD (V.O.)
When I first moved here, the phone number they gave me was one digit away from the number of a pizza place....

CUT TO: Richard answering the phone with a look of exasperation.

                    CALLER (O.S.)
Hi, I'd like to order a large pie with everything and two medium Cokes.

                    RICHARD
Be there in five minutes.

CUT TO: Richard listening to the desperate voice.

                    RICHARD (V.O.)
So I had the phone company change it. Unfortunately, my new number is one digit away from the Suicide Prevention Hotline.... And I don't have the heart to tell

> these people they have the wrong number.
> That could be the final thing that pushes
> them over the edge.

INT. A SUBWAY TRAIN - DAY

Seated on a crowded subway train, Richard lets his gaze drift from one face to the next—like living Diane Arbus portraits.

> RICHARD (V.O.)
> Once you develop a daily routine, you start
> to notice the same faces over and over—as
> familiar as your own relatives yet you don't
> even know their names. Like characters in
> a movie who appear in only one scene, they
> have no separate lives outside this train.

An OLD LADY with her stockings rolled down around her knees like two cinnamon doughnuts...

> RICHARD (V.O.) (cont.)
> Her favorite pastimes are clipping coupons
> and complaining about her ungrateful
> children.

The ITALIAN STALLION, with his black hair slicked back, as shiny as a vinyl record...

> RICHARD (V.O.) (cont.)
> He's saving up to buy a car with the profits
> from 46 stolen radios.

The JUNIOR EXECUTRIX in her Evan-Picone suit and Reeboks, like a sparrow ready to flee at the first hint of danger...

> RICHARD (V.O.) (cont.)
> She's thinking about taking assertiveness training, but can't decide.

A MAINTENANCE MAN in his green uniform with a fat wad of keys on his belt...

> RICHARD (V.O.) (cont.)
> Ask him the time and he'll tell you how a watch works. Guys with keys on their belts tend to be know-it-alls.

A MIDDLE-AGED WOMAN, her skin stretched so tight around her face, she's frog-eyed with a look of perpetual astonishment...

> RICHARD (V.O.) (cont.)
> Her face has been lifted more times than a blind guy's wallet on the D train.

A PSYCHOPATH dressed like a load of dirty laundry and chuckling into his fist at some unseen comedian...

> RICHARD (V.O.) (cont.)
> His breath is so corrosive it could skin the enamel off your teeth.

Richard examines his own reflection in the window.

> RICHARD (V.O.) (cont.)
> A timid nobody tormented by voices who lives in fear of...

EXT. A CITY PARK - DAY

Richard sits on a bench, feeding the pigeons. He arranges the bread crumbs in a complicated pattern on the pavement and watches the birds march in labyrinthine motions.

> RICHARD (V.O.)
> ...everything. Fear of death. Fear of life. Fear of spontaneous human combustion.

A male JOGGER in his 40s approaches in SLOW MOTION.

> RICHARD (V.O.) (cont.)
> When I was eight years old, there was a total eclipse of the sun. In school they warned us not to look or else you'd go blind, and I was so terrified that all day I kept my eyes glued to the ground in fear I'd accidentally catch a glimpse of light and my eyeballs would burst into flames.

YOUNG RICHARD, eight years old, walks by with a book bag slung over his shoulder, staring intently at the ground, both hands shading his eyes.

> RICHARD (V.O.) (cont.)
> I'd read that during a solar eclipse, incidents of spontaneous human combustion increased by over fifty percent.

A LITTLE OLD LADY wearing wraparound sunglasses strolls by with a portable fire extinguisher sticking out of her purse.

> RICHARD (V.O.) (cont.)
> I imagine it starts suddenly, with a heavy, burning ache in the chest.

His face flush, his breathing shallow, the jogger slows to a walk and places a hand on his chest.

> RICHARD (V.O.) (cont.)
> Then the skin starts to tingle, as the tiny, ticklish licks of flame snap at the tips of your fingers and toes.

Confused and alarmed, the jogger shakes his hands back and forth. His heart is audibly POUNDING now, his face twisted in panic.

> RICHARD (V.O.) (cont.)
> Until, in a crackling explosion of flame, it's over...

In a flash, the jogger is consumed by fire. Richard squints and shields his eyes from the light. When he looks back, there's a smoking pile of ashes where the jogger had been.

> RICHARD (V.O.) (cont.)
> And all that's left are the brand-new $800 Nikes.

A BAG LADY wanders up to the jogger's remains. With a stick she pokes at the smoldering embers and pulls out the clean white running shoes. Carefully she brushes away some ash, stuffs the shoes into her bag, and shuffles away.

> RICHARD (V.O.) (cont.)
> Why do people run if it makes them feel awful? So they can live longer? So life will feel awful but at least it'll last a long time? A man will do anything out of fear.... Personally I don't believe in exercise. I think your heart has only so many beats in it, and I don't intend on speeding them up. If I wanted my heart to beat faster, I'd just drink stronger coffee.

INT. THE VIDEO STORE - DAY

Richard is tediously shelving tape boxes.

> RICHARD (V.O.)
> Maybe I should've gone to business school. I'd be on Wall Street making six figures by now.... No, that's not me. Wearing a suit and tie all day in an office with spiteful, backstabbing coworkers. I'd just be miserable.... Yeah, right. Like I'm really having a ball now.

INT. A SUBWAY TRAIN - DAY

Richard stands on a subway train, caught in the crush of rush-hour COMMUTERS, the tension of bodies pressed too close together. A large, menacing MAN shatters the uneasy silence.

> MAN
> I really value my personal space, man!

Richard and the others standing nearby nervously try to give him some room.

> RICHARD (V.O.)
> Nothing can make you feel more alone than being crowded together with a bunch of strangers.

The shifting of bodies has placed Richard in close proximity to a BEAUTIFUL WOMAN seated near the door. He glances at her and sees the woman dressed only in her underwear. She looks up suddenly, he turns away, and she's fully clothed again.

> RICHARD (V.O.) (cont.)
> It's been so long since I touched another

human being. Sometimes a casual jostle on the train...

The woman gets up and accidentally brushes against Richard as the train jolts to a stop. He nearly swoons with stifled longing at the unexpected contact.

INT. THE VIDEO STORE - DAY

Keith, Richard, and Tim are lined up at the counter, chins in hands, listening to the giant mosquito whine of the overhead fluorescent lighting.

> TIM
> I hate when they walk up and you can tell exactly what they had for lunch.

> KEITH
> I hate when they ask for something we don't have but they don't believe you. They say, "Are you *sure?*"

> TIM
> Or they ask you to check "the back room."

> KEITH
> Yeah, the secret room where we hide all the really good stuff.

A loud, corpulent woman, MRS. DELOACH, charges up to the counter.

> MRS. DELOACH
> That show you gave me? I hated it!

> KEITH
> Good morning, Mrs. D.

> MRS. DELOACH
> All the people in this show be dead! I don't wanna be looking at dead people! Gimme something else!

Keith searches through a stack of unshelved tape boxes.

> KEITH
> Let's see... How about this? Michael Douglas, Kathleen Turner—they're both alive.

> MRS. DELOACH
> Oh, that's old! I seen that about a million times!

Richard pushes a box across the counter.

> RICHARD
> This just came in.

> KEITH
> Yeah, it's an early Spike Lee film about these two—

> MRS. DELOACH
> That's black and white! I don't watch no movie in black and white!
> *(to Richard)*
> You trying to make me watch black and white?!

Richard swallows and shakes his head.

INT. A SUBWAY TRAIN - DAY

Richard stares across the aisle at the same beautiful woman he saw before.

                    RICHARD (V.O.)
          It must be wonderful to wake up in the
          morning and see that face in the mirror
          each day and know that it's yours.

The woman looks up at Richard briefly, then down again with the barest hint of a smile.

                    RICHARD (V.O.) (cont.)
          Oh, my God. Was that a—? Yes! She smiled!
          I can't believe it. She actually smiled at me.
          God, I feel like we're engaged. I want to
          know everything about her.

INT. A DETECTIVE'S OFFICE - DAY

In BLACK & WHITE, Richard sits in the office of Spade & Archer, 1940s film noir detectives. Seated across from him, bathed in shadows, a cigarette dangling from his lip, is the DETECTIVE, rummaging through his desk for a lighter.

                    DETECTIVE
          This dame—you want me to follow her, I
          suppose.

                    RICHARD
          That's right. I want to find out everything—
          where she lives, where she works, who her
          friends—

                    DETECTIVE
          Say, have you got a light?

                    RICHARD
          Uh, no, sorry, I don't...

                    DETECTIVE
          Never mind.

The detective pulls out a revolver and fires a single bullet across the tip of his cigarette. Richard jumps at the sudden EXPLOSION; the detective calmly takes a puff.

INT. A SUBWAY TRAIN - DAY

The SCREECH of the subway jolts Richard back to reality. The woman is gone, and he looks around to figure out where he is.

                    RICHARD (V.O.)
          Maybe I think too much. Maybe I just—oh,
          damn. I missed my stop again.

INT. THE VIDEO STORE - DAY

Richard checks in a camcorder being returned by a customer, then joins Keith and Tim leaning over the counter, chins in hands, bored out of their minds.

                    TIM
          Teen sex comedies.

                    KEITH
          Teen slasher films.

                    TIM
          Sexy teen slasher buddies.

                    KEITH
          Sexy teen slasher cop buddies.

                    TIM
          Cop-on-the-edge buddies.

KEITH
"He's a cop on the edge!"

TIM
Chasing drug kingpins.

KEITH
South American drug kingpins.

RICHARD
And serial killers.

TIM
Okay, sexy teen slasher cop buddies—

KEITH
Cop-on-the-edge buddies.

TIM
Sexy teen slasher cop-on-the-edge buddies chasing South American drug kingpin serial killers.

KEITH
I think we got it.

RICHARD
The feel-good hit of the year.

KEITH
Don't forget the Motown song in the credits.

TIM
Jeez, I'm getting so tired of that.

RICHARD
I'm getting tired of Vietnam War movies.

                    TIM
          I've seen so many Vietnam movies, I feel
          like I was there.

                    KEITH
          I think I have post-traumatic stress disor-
          der.

INT. RICHARD'S APARTMENT - NIGHT

Zapping through channels with the remote, Richard is mesmerized by the images on his TV screen.

                    RICHARD (V.O.)
          This is the global village, and I am the
          global village idiot.

                    VOICES FROM THE TV (O.S.)
          ...Ellie May is washing her critters in the
          cement pond!— Women who still love the
          men who tried to murder them: That's our
          focus on today's— This lovely ceramic don-
          key, just $19.95, makes a perfect center-
          piece—

                    RICHARD (V.O.)
                      (overlapping)
          Never underestimate what a person will do
          to get himself on TV. A man with a camera
          is a man with power.

                    VOICES FROM THE TV (O.S.)
          ...Cartoons for $1,000. This cub reporter
          was the canine companion of TV's crime-
          fighting Underdog.

                        RICHARD
                Who is Sweet Polly Purebred?

                        VOICES FROM THE TV (O.S.)
                Who is Lois Lane?

Richard rolls his eyes in scorn.

                        VOICES FROM THE TV (O.S.) (cont.)
                No. The correct response is: Who is Sweet
                Polly Purebred?

                        RICHARD (V.O.)
                Everyday life is bland and predictable, but
                TV is like seeing through the eyes of God.
                How can reality compete with that? If a tree
                falls in the forest and they don't show it on
                TV, did it really happen? No, reality is
                what happens when your TV is busted.

EXT. A CITY SIDEWALK - DAY

Prowling the sidewalk with a camcorder, Richard tapes random PASSERSBY. Every person he sees gives him a curious, expectant glance.

                        RICHARD (V.O.)
                The camera gives me life. They look at me
                now. I don't feel invisible. Somehow hav-
                ing a camera turns even me into a magnetic
                personality.

Suddenly, across the street, he spots the beautiful woman from the subway.

                        RICHARD (V.O.) (cont.)
                Oh, my God. It's her! I don't believe it.

Dodging traffic, Richard hurries across the street and records her approach. As she gets closer, he lowers the camcorder and stands, paralyzed, with a nervous half-smile. But she breezes right past him without a glance, and Richard turns to watch her go, staring with adoration and despair.

> RICHARD (V.O.) (cont.)
> Maybe she didn't see me.... No, that's not it. She did it on purpose. She hates me. Damn!... But I can't give up. I have to meet her.

EXT. A CITY SIDEWALK - DAY

Richard stands in the shadowy recess of a building, his body fidgeting, his face a mask of frozen longing. In his mind he replays the videotaped image of the subway woman over and over.

> RICHARD (V.O.)
> At least she didn't slap me or spit in my face, so she must like me a little, right? Maybe that's something to build on.... I've sacrificed my lunch hour every day to wait for her to walk by. I live for every glimpse. I imagine her stumbling on that grate and falling into my arms. I think I'm a little obsessed with her.... But maybe she's thinking the same thing. Maybe she's just shy. Maybe she even likes me too but wants me to make the first move. Yesterday she held that glance just a fraction of a second longer than usual. Her eyes were practically begging me to say hi. And her smile—almost a grin, really— God, that proves it! This time I'll walk right up to her and she'll say...

> RICHARD (V.O.) & WOMAN (O.S.)
> *(in unison)*
> ...I've been watching you for so long.

The woman appears in front of Richard and smiles.

> RICHARD
> I've been meaning to say hi but I don't even know your name.

> WOMAN
> I've been wanting to meet you too, but I was too embarrassed to say anything. Isn't that silly?

> RICHARD (V.O.)
> Then we'll both laugh and I'll say...

> RICHARD
> I'm glad one of us finally broke the ice.

CUT TO: Richard anxiously lying in wait. He fixes his hair in a window reflection, then looks down the sidewalk to see the woman approaching. Earnestly he practices his line.

> RICHARD (V.O.)
> I've been meaning to say hi but I don't even know your name.... I've been meaning to say hi but I don't even know your name....

Finally he steps out onto the sidewalk, trying too hard to seem casual, and blocks the woman's path.

> RICHARD
> I've been meaning to say hi but—

She's startled and tries to go around him, but no matter which way she turns, Richard jumps in front of her.

> RICHARD (cont.)
> I've been— I've been meaning to say—

Now she's getting panicky. She tries to make an end-run around him, but their feet get tangled and they both fall to the pavement. With a cry of distress, she scrambles to her feet and flees down the sidewalk.

> RICHARD (cont.)
> Wait, I'm sorry, I... Damn.

Richard stares after her, forlorn.

INT. THE VIDEO STORE - DAY

Richard places a tape in the store's VCR, demonstrating it to an angry customer, MR. SPERLING, while Tim watches sedately.

> TIM
> Looks fine to me, dude.

> MR. SPERLING
> I'm telling you, it was jumping! I couldn't even watch it, it was so bad.

> TIM
> We're gonna have to charge you.

> MR. SPERLING
> But why? I didn't even see it!

> TIM
> Not our fault. Nothing wrong with it.

MR. SPERLING
I can't believe this!

TIM
It's not a question of believing or not believing, man. It's not faith or metaphysics. It's a hard fact. Store policy. Caveat emptor. Shit like that.

Richard starts to write up his charges.

MR. SPERLING
Oh, come on! Give me a break!

TIM
A break? You want a break? Why should I give you a break, man? When was the last time anyone gave me a break, huh?

The man tries to respond but Tim cuts him off.

TIM (cont.)
Listen, I sympathize, dude, but if I start giving breaks to every guy with a complaint about this fine establishment, I'm gonna be out on the street. And I'm not about to jeopardize my lucrative Video Shack pension plan to save you two bucks, okay?

MR. SPERLING
It's not the two bucks—it's the principle, okay?!

TIM
(to Richard)
It's always the cheapskates who stand on principle.

MR. SPERLING
Hey! I heard that! I want to talk to the manager!

TIM
He's at lunch.

MR. SPERLING
Well, there must be somebody in charge here!

TIM
You're looking at him, dude.

MR. SPERLING
You're the manager?

TIM
Acting manager.

RICHARD
Hard to believe, isn't it?

MR. SPERLING
(*apoplectic*)
I won't stand for this!

TIM
(*to Richard*)
Here we go.

MR. SPERLING
I've been a loyal customer in this store—I won't be treated this way!

                    TIM
              (to Richard)
         I hate it when they whine.
              (to Mr. Sperling)
         Come on, man, you know that's not gonna
         work here. Have a little self-respect, huh?

Mr. Sperling takes out a scrap of paper and starts scribbling.

                MR. SPERLING
         That's it! I'm taking down your name. You
         picked on the wrong guy this time!

                    TIM
         Wilson. Conventional spelling.

                MR. SPERLING
         I know people in this company! I can make
         your life a living hell!

                    TIM
         Too late.

                MR. SPERLING
         Smart-aleck kid! That's the last time I set
         foot in this place!

                    TIM
         Promise?

Mr. Sperling stuffs the paper into his pocket, slams his money on the counter, and heads for the door.

                   RICHARD
         That was impressive.

                    TIM

Him or me?

                    RICHARD

Both.

                    TIM

We get a lot of practice.

                    RICHARD

Aren't you worried?

                    TIM

About him? Nah. He's a regular. He does that every week.

On his way in the door, Keith passes the angry customer.

                    KEITH

Hi, Mr. Sperling.

                    RICHARD

How can you stand waiting on these people day after day?

                    TIM

Well, basically, I just try to think of this place as a zoo. And all of these people you see—these are my animals. And every day I have to feed them or they'll die.

                    RICHARD

And that works?

                    TIM

Sure. When you toss a slab of meat in the tiger's cage, you don't expect the tiger to thank you, right? You don't expect the monkeys and the wallabies to show you respect. They're just animals. So put yourself in that mind space and you'll never be offended by their behavior.... It's just pure survival, man.

A WOMAN carrying her VCR interrupts Keith behind the counter.

WOMAN
Hey! Show me what to press if I want to record a show.

TIM
(to Richard)
And don't ever try discussing technology with them. They just stare at you with these eyes like little blank TV screens.

RICHARD
Some people are so helpless, you wonder how they manage to survive in the world.

TIM
Sometimes I wish life was more like some TV nature show, and all these people were a herd of gazelles. That way the slow ones would all get eaten by lions.

RICHARD
Maybe they should consider releasing a few humans back into the wild.

INT. AN OFFICE BUILDING - DAY

In the sterile lobby of an office tower, an attractive YOUNG

WOMAN holding a briefcase faces a bank of three elevators. Richard stands a short distance away. They glance at each other furtively. The lighted numerals over the door of Elevator #2 indicate its approach; a BELL RINGS and the door slides open. They reach it together and Richard hesitates with an awkward step, allowing the woman to enter first. A PORTLY MAN who looks like Alfred Hitchcock rushes up to the door as it closes.

Inside, Richard steals a glance at the woman staring up at the floor numbers. She does the same to him. Outside in the lobby, the portly man checks his watch, as he's joined by SEVERAL OTHERS. The woman gives Richard a sultry look, as he silently pulls a pad of paper and pen from his jacket. He writes something, pockets the pad, then quickly pries open the door with his fingers and jams the pen into the crack. The elevator jolts to a stop. The woman watches expectantly as Richard turns to her.

Out in the lobby, it's business as usual. The lighted numbers above the door of Elevator #2 indicate that it's stuck between floors. Elevator #1 arrives; the assembled crowd climbs aboard. A moment later, the door of Elevator #3 opens and several PASSENGERS step out. Above the door of Elevator #2, the lights remain suspended, while inside, the SOUNDS of EXERTION and HEAVY BREATHING are heard. Finally, the lighted numbers over the second door slowly begin to creep downward. A small CROWD gathers, preparing to board. A BELL RINGS and the door slides open.

CUT TO: Reality. The woman casually exits the elevator. Richard, filled with longing and dejection, follows.

INT. RICHARD'S APARTMENT - NIGHT

Sitting on the floor with a pen and a newspaper, Richard reads the personal ads. He crosses off each one as it's rejected.

RICHARD (V.O.)
No... No... Definitely no... "Single white female looking for a man who cares about more than a pretty face." Maybe... No... "Single white female, weight proportionate to height." What the hell does that mean?

Richard leans back and sighs with hopelessness.

RICHARD (V.O.) (cont.)
They say there's somebody out there for everyone, but how am I supposed to find her? There are five billion people in the world....

He grabs a calculator and starts figuring.

RICHARD (V.O.) (cont.)
If half of them are female, that's 2½ billion. Subtract the ones who are too young or too old or already married. That leaves 275 million available women. So, if I go out twice a week, every week, for the rest of my life, to find Miss Right it should take no more than... 2.5 million years.

He exhales wearily and starts to get up.

RICHARD
Better get started.

INT. RICHARD'S APARTMENT - DAY

Freshly showered and shirtless, Richard stands in front of his closet, paralyzed because he can't decide what to wear. He pulls out a shirt, sniffs the underarm, then puts it back. He pulls out another, sniffs the underarm, and decides it's acceptable.

INT. A SUBWAY TRAIN - DAY

Richard sits on the subway, reading from a book called *Modern Dating* and jotting down notes on a piece of paper.

> RICHARD (V.O.)
> (reading)
> Always smile and ask questions. Act interested in what she says.

He writes it down, then practices softly to himself.

> RICHARD
> Hi, how are you? So, what do you do for a living? Really? That's interesting.

He jots down a note, then reads some more.

> RICHARD (V.O.)
> (reading)
> Make frequent eye contact. Compliment her appearance: "That's a very pretty sweater you're wearing."

> RICHARD
> That's a very pretty sweater you're wearing.

> RICHARD (V.O.)
> "You have beautiful eyes."

> RICHARD
> You know, you have beautiful eyes. That's a very pretty sweater you're wearing.

A WOMAN sitting nearby looks at Richard quizzically as he self-consciously smoothes his hair and scrapes his teeth with a finger.

EXT. A MOVIE THEATER - DUSK

Richard loiters outside a movie theater with a single red rose in his hand. Every few moments, he smoothes his hair or looks nervously at his crib sheet. He breaks into a weak smile each time a WOMAN veers toward him. Then, as she veers away, he frowns and smoothes his hair again.

> RICHARD (V.O.)
> Wait, is that her? No...

One after another, WOMEN of every shape and size walk past without stopping, while Richard earnestly rehearses his lines.

> RICHARD (V.O.) (cont.)
> Hi, how are you? I'm Richard. Hi, my name is Richard, how are you?... Oh God, I hope it's not her— Phew. Is that her? She's not bad. I hope— No.

It's starting to get late. The lights are on above the theater and a CROWD is lining up outside, as Richard's anxiety grows.

> RICHARD (V.O.) (cont.)
> Oh God, I'm dying out here....

CUT TO: Richard standing outside the theater. The crowd is gone, the sun has set, and Richard is despondent.

> RICHARD (V.O.) (cont.)
> She's not coming. I should've known. She

probably took one look at me and kept on walking.

A WOMAN appears. She seems to be looking for someone. Richard is hopeful. But then she runs into the warm embrace of another man waiting outside the theater and they enter arm in arm. With a sigh, Richard turns and begins the long, slow walk home.

> RICHARD (V.O.) (cont.)
> What did I do wrong? I keep going over every second of our call, trying to figure out where I screwed up. The phone rings; I answer it. She introduces herself, says she got my number from the ad. I say, "Hello, it's nice to—"

Richard stops.

> RICHARD (V.O.) (cont.)
> Oh, my God. Hi. I should've said "hi"! Oh, shit! "Hello"?! What the hell was I thinking?! Nobody says "hello" these days! It's "hi." Everyone says "hi"! I can't believe I said "hello," like a schoolmarm. Idiot.

He continues walking.

> RICHARD (V.O.) (cont.)
> I don't care. I don't need her. I can still have fun.

EXT. AN AMUSEMENT PARK - NIGHT

Richard sits all alone on a speeding roller coaster, bug-eyed and stone-faced, like a psychotic Buster Keaton.

EXT. A CITY SIDEWALK - NIGHT

Stoop-shouldered and brooding, Richard walks home. He gazes with longing at each WOMAN who passes, seductive and graceful, moving in SLOW MOTION.

> RICHARD (V.O.)
> Women have it all figured out. They know exactly what to say, how to look, what to wear. Exactly what to do to get under our skin. Men are powerless against them. And they complain about equality. Equality! Women who want equality with men lack ambition. They already have such mastery over us—where will it end? I just don't get it.... And that's another part of their power. They're so mysterious. All a woman has to do is smile at me and I'm her slave for life.

INT. RICHARD'S APARTMENT - NIGHT

Richard sits in the dark watching TV, while Travis stalks across the floor, hovering behind him like a guilty conscience.

> RICHARD
> ...I'd be willing to marry the first woman I meet who doesn't treat me like scum.

> TRAVIS
> You're hopeless.

> RICHARD
> I just need to connect with someone.

> TRAVIS
> You don't make any impression at all. You just take up space.

RICHARD
I want to be able to say I changed the life of another person.

TRAVIS
You could light up a room by leaving it.

RICHARD
I just want someone to know who I am before I explode.

TRAVIS
None of your T-shirts say anything.

RICHARD
Hey, if I wanted to be insulted, I'd move back home and be insulted by an expert.... I'm just not a warm person. Maybe I should be warmer.

TRAVIS
I don't think your temperature is the problem, Dave.

The PHONE RINGS and Travis goes over to answer it, but Richard jumps up and stops him.

RICHARD
Wait! Let the machine get it! It's probably her! She's calling to apologize. I knew it!

Richard hovers over the answering machine expectantly as it CLICKS into action.

RICHARD'S VOICE
(from machine)
Hello...

                    TRAVIS
                  (scornfully)
"Hello"?

                RICHARD'S VOICE
                 (from machine)
          ...This is Richard Freeman. Please leave your
          message after the beep.

The BEEP is quickly followed by the CLICK of a phone being
hung up. At first Richard doesn't understand what's happened.
Then, in a panic, he grabs the receiver.

                    RICHARD
          Hello? Hello? Hello?!

Deflated, Richard hangs up the phone and slumps onto his
mattress. Travis leans over him and whispers in his ear.

                    TRAVIS
          You're making this seem a lot more com-
          plicated than it is, Dave.

                    RICHARD
          What are you talking about?

                    TRAVIS
          What every woman wants is a man who'll
          share with her. What every man wants is a
          woman who'll protect his ego.

                    RICHARD
                  (after a pause)
          Yeah, that's great, but it's too long to fit on
          a T-shirt.

INT. THE VIDEO STORE - DAY

Richard is desultorily shelving boxes on the floor while customers scan the shelves. Keith is behind the counter conducting inventory.

> RICHARD (V.O.)
> They work hard all day to put their kids through college so they won't end up working in a video store.... Then they race home for another long night of falling asleep in front of the TV and not dreaming...

Richard reaches the adult video section, where several MEN are trying to appear invisible.

> MR. PEARSON (O.S.)
> How many?! That's impossible. You must have miscounted. Do it again.

> RICHARD (V.O.)
> ...Even sex is nothing but a spectator sport.

Keith drags himself out of the office, exasperated.

EXT. A CITY STREET - DAY

Richard is still stuck in traffic. The clock on the dash of his rental car reads 11:38 and he's starting to get nervous. A car up ahead is trying to merge, but Richard won't let him in. The DRIVER HONKS, and Richard HONKS right back.

> RICHARD (V.O.)
> This guy's not getting in. Forget it, buddy, this is too important. I don't even see you....

INT. THE VIDEO STORE - DAY

Richard stands behind the counter, his back to the store, blankly watching a movie on the TV screen. An irritated CUSTOMER tries to get his attention by shaking a videotape box in front of his face.

> RICHARD
> (*surly*)
> What?

Richard takes the man's box and sullenly fills his order.

> RICHARD (V.O.)
> Don't make eye contact. Refuse to acknowledge their existence. I am the forest primeval. I am the swamp at the pit of the world....

> RICHARD
> That's $3.98. Would you like a bag?

> RICHARD (V.O.) (cont.)
> I am the person you see every day whose eyes you try to avoid. I am Shiva, the god of destruction....

> RICHARD
> Next!

EXT. A BEACH - NIGHT

Richard and KRISTINE, a radiant woman with long blond hair, stroll hand in hand across the beautiful moonlit sand.

> RICHARD (V.O.)
> I'd never met anyone like her. We liked the

same movies, Italian restaurants—we talked about everything under the sun.... How strange and wonderful it was not to be frightened by a woman.

Suddenly, from nowhere, a tremendous wave CRASHES onto the beach, hurling Richard and Kristine to the ground, submerging them in a rush of ocean water and foam.

> RICHARD (V.O.) (cont.)
> Until that night, when the wave came, and washed her out to sea.

Richard, coughing and gasping for air, staggers to his feet and scans the beach, but Kristine is nowhere in sight. Bewildered, he turns his eyes to the sea and gazes forlornly after her.

> RICHARD (V.O.) (cont.)
> Soldiers who've lost a limb in battle say they feel like it's still there.... Every movie I see is about her and me. Sometimes I think she never really existed—she was just a ghost or an angel. Anyway, I never saw her again.

INT. A RESTAURANT - NIGHT

Richard sits at a table with his latest in a series of disastrous blind dates.

> RICHARD (V.O.)
> Dating is a lot like playing the lottery. You know you're never going to win, but you just keep on buying tickets.

Her name is MARILLA ODOM. She and Richard stare at the

ceiling, the walls, the waitress, anything but each other's eyes, in the agonizing silence of self-consciousness.

                    RICHARD
So...

                    MARILLA
So...

                    RICHARD (V.O.)
Every single thought I've ever had in my life has vanished from my brain. My mind is a perfect vacuum. Oh God, get me out of here. I can't think of anything to— Wait! Compliment her!

                    RICHARD
That's a very pretty sweater you're wearing.

                    MARILLA
Oh, thank you.

                    RICHARD
              (after a long pause)
Did you make it yourself?

                    MARILLA
No. I bought it.
              (long pause)
You know. In a store.

                    RICHARD
Oh.
              (long pause)
A sweater store?

MARILLA
A— what? No—just a, you know... regular store.

RICHARD (V.O.)
God, why do I keep doing this to myself?

MARILLA
I noticed your sneakers.

RICHARD
What?

MARILLA
Those. Are they... running shoes?

RICHARD
Oh. Yeah.

MARILLA
Do you exercise?

RICHARD
Uh... well, I do a lot of pacing.

MARILLA
Pacing?

RICHARD
And worrying. Pacing and worrying.

MARILLA
Oh.

RICHARD
Guess that doesn't really count.... What about you?

MARILLA
What?

RICHARD
Do you exer—?

MARILLA
Oh! No.... I like to cook.

RICHARD
Oh, really? Me, too.

MARILLA
You like to cook?

RICHARD
Oh. No, I meant— Well, sometimes, like, you know... toast.

MARILLA
Oh.... So, what do you eat?

RICHARD
Mainly, uh... anything frozen in a box.

RICHARD (V.O.)
Oh God, get me out of here.

CUT TO: Same restaurant, same table, but a new date: AMY ROSEN.

AMY
...After graduation, my parents sent me on a trip around the world. It was okay, I guess. Next year I want to go someplace different.

RICHARD
Uh... you said on the phone that you're an artist?

AMY
Uh-huh. I'm a nail sculptress.

RICHARD
A nail—?

AMY
Nail sculptress. You know, fingernails. See?

She shows him her fingernails, on each of which is carved a tiny portrait in relief.

AMY (cont.)
Sometimes toenails, except if they're gnarly.

RICHARD
That's, uh— Who are—?

AMY
That's my parents, my uncle Lou, my boyfriend—I mean, *ex*-boyfriend—Steven, and my cat Princess. She's Siamese.

RICHARD
That's.... Are those really your nails?

AMY
Nah, these are my show nails. They're acrylic. You think I'd hack up my dress nails like that?...

Richard smiles with feigned interest, but his mind is elsewhere.

RICHARD (V.O.)
In every blind date, there comes a moment when you start mentally calculating how much time courtesy requires that you wait before pulling the plug on this thing.

AMY
...My cousin Stacy, she does calligraphy—you know, weddings and stuff? She makes a fortune....

RICHARD (V.O.)
Kirk to Enterprise. Energize... Energize...

CUT TO: Same restaurant, same table, DARCY MYERS, a woman as stable as Jell-O. She's wearing a button that says "I'm a mess" and speaks without pausing for breath.

DARCY
I hate these blind dates. There's so much tension. I never know what to say. I used to be agoraphobic but now I'm the opposite of agoraphobic. It's like, I have a panic attack if I don't get enough stimulation. Do you know if there's a name for that? I don't know. My therapist says I became a psych major because I was looking for someone to blame. Do you think that's true?

RICHARD
You were a psych major?

DARCY
No way! You too? So what's your favorite ego defense mechanism?

RICHARD
Probably denial.

DARCY
Really? I've never been into denial. But I guess if I was, I wouldn't admit it.
(she laughs self-consciously)
Oh, my God, have you ever had an out-of-body experience? I have....

CUT TO: Same restaurant, same table, BETSY BONDARCHUK, wearing big round orange earrings and self-conscious hair.

RICHARD (V.O.)
Look at that hair. And those earrings—my God, they look exactly like Ritz crackers....

BETSY
I love Tom Cruise. He's so cool, and not conceited at all.

RICHARD (V.O.)
Man, I could really go for some Ritz crackers.

CUT TO: Same restaurant, same table, CYNTHIA VANDERSLICE.

CYNTHIA
I suspect Salinger was attempting to lampoon the futility of crypto-lesbian symbiosis in the cultural void of pre-postmodernism by means of this dichotomy between a simple axiomatic deconstruction of proto-Marxist textural symbols and the radical feminist archetypes of the Jungian dialectic...

                    RICHARD (V.O.)
                      (overlapping)
        I couldn't pay attention to what she was
        saying because there was a long, thin strand
        of saliva dancing back and forth between
        her teeth, and no matter how hard I tried,
        I couldn't take my eyes off it. It was like
        watching a lava lamp.

CUT TO: Amy Rosen. Richard is munching on a celery stick.

                         AMY
        Anyway, the next guy I went out with, he
        turned out to be a queer.

                    RICHARD (V.O.)
        I wonder if the chewing sound outside my
        head is as loud as the chewing sound inside
        my head.

CUT TO: Darcy Myers.

                        DARCY
        ...The fact that I can kill myself anytime is
        what keeps me alive. It's like my personal
        choice, you know? But actually today was a
        pretty good day. I hardly felt suicidal at all.
        I used to be a very negative person, but
        then I took this personality workshop and
        it totally turned my life around. My thera-
        pist says I'm too hard on myself. Did I
        mention that I'm seeing a therapist? It's
        only twice a week, but it helps sustain me. I
        really should have been a dancer—that's
        what everyone tells me. Actually, no one's
        ever said that to me. I just made it up. I'm

sorry for rambling. Whenever I get nervous I talk a lot....

RICHARD
Whenever I get nervous I hum the theme from *Star Wars*.

DARCY
...I've been having the strangest dreams lately. My therapist says....

CUT TO: Betsy Bondarchuk.

BETSY
...Like when you eat a really hot pizza? And you get those little strings hanging from the roof of your mouth? I think that's...

RICHARD (V.O.)
Everything tastes great when it sits on a Ritz.

CUT TO: Same restaurant, same table, EMMA NUSSBAUM.

EMMA
...I guess I've always been an other-directed sort of person. But I feel really good about myself, too. I think beauty comes from the inside. I see it as sort of an inner light, like a glow—not a glow, exactly, but like an inner wholeness, a peaceful—a shining light, like a shining, glowing peaceful thing, like an orb, like a glowing orb, you know?

RICHARD
Yeah. Exactly.

                    RICHARD (V.O.)
                Oh, God, make this stop.

CUT TO: Darcy Myers, frantically fanning herself.

                        DARCY
                Oh, God. It's happening—

                       RICHARD
    What?

                        DARCY
                A panic attack. I'm having—oh, God! I told
                you, if I don't get enough stimulation—

She checks her pulse.

                       RICHARD
                What should I do?

                        DARCY
                Stimulation! I need— Some kind of— Any-
                thing, do anything!

In a panic, Richard tries to give her emergency stimulation by sticking a tomato on his nose like a clown and making shadow puppets against the wall.

CUT TO: Marilla Odom. Amazingly, she and Richard seem to be hitting it off. She's starting to laugh at his jokes.

                       MARILLA
                What do you do when you're not writing?

                       RICHARD
                Uh, mainly I stand in lines. I'm like a pro-
                fessional line stander.

She laughs.

> RICHARD (V.O.)
> This seems to be going pretty well. At least she's not a psychopath. What a relief.

> MARILLA
> Did I mention that I'm a witch?

CUT TO: Amy Rosen

> AMY
> ...And then in third grade, Daniel Melnick said he liked me, but I found out he liked Mindy Goldman even more and I was, like, totally crushed, you know?...

> RICHARD (V.O.)
> *(singing)*
> Flintstones, meet the Flintstones, they're a modern Stone Age fa-mi-ly....

CUT TO: Darcy Myers.

> DARCY
> ...Don't get me wrong, my cat is very special to me, but I think if I'm reincarnated, I'd rather come back as a sea otter...

> RICHARD (V.O.)
> *(overlapping)*
> I can't believe she's still going. My God, I think she's using up all the oxygen in the room— I'm starting to feel lightheaded. I— I can't breathe....

Gasping for breath, Richard grasps the table for support.

DARCY
Is something wrong?

RICHARD
I'll be right back.

Richard gets up and hurries from the table.

CUT TO: The men's room. Richard sits on a toilet with his head between his legs, pale and sweating.

RICHARD (V.O.)
Oh, God. If this were a movie, it'd be over by now.

CUT TO: Amy Rosen, showing Richard pictures from her vacation. He stares with glazed eyes and a frozen smile.

AMY
This is a picture of some mountain in Italy, but it's really foggy so you can't see it. And this is a picture of my cousin Leo in Africa, but you can't tell it's him, it's too dark.

RICHARD (V.O.)
Is that the last one? Please, God.

AMY
And this is a picture of my uncle Roy in Hawaii...

RICHARD (V.O.)
No, still going.

                    AMY
    ...but he moved at the last second so all you
    can see is his foot.

Suddenly Richard is rising from his seat and floating out of his body. Amy continues showing him her pictures, but her voice sounds like it's underwater.

                 RICHARD (V.O.)
    Oh, no. It's happening again....

His transparent form floats up to the ceiling and hovers over the table. Richard looks down at himself and Amy before drifting away into darkness.

              RICHARD (V.O.) (cont.)
    I want to know something eternal. I want
    to feel alive inside, smash the wall at the
    end of the world, tamper with the universe.
    I want to be an icon—Shakespeare or Robin
    Hood, the Mona Lisa, mon amour....

EXT. A DESERT HIGHWAY - DUSK

In a '65 Mustang convertible, Richard is cruising a desert highway with the MONA LISA by his side—not the painting but the woman, her long black hair flowing in the breeze and an indescribable smile on her face. The RADIO is playing a Motown song.

                 RICHARD (V.O.)
    ...I want to go cruising with Mona Lisa. I
    want to show her America—just me and
    Mona, the open road, and Smokey on the
    radio. And I'll toss a little glance her way,

                    and she'll smile that little smile of hers.
                    She won't say anything... but I'll know.

Mona Lisa dons a pair of Ray-Bans and leans back in her seat, as the sun sets over the desert mountains and Richard cruises into the night.

INT. THE RESTAURANT - NIGHT

Amy's lips are still moving as Richard slowly returns to reality.

                              AMY
                    ...So what do you think? Huh?

                            RICHARD
                    What?

                              AMY
                    I asked if you're ready to go. Why are you
                    looking at me that way?

                            RICHARD
                    Oh. I— I'm sorry.

Richard knows he's been a jerk. He and Amy get up to leave.

                              AMY
                    God, you guys are all alike. I knew this
                    would be a mistake.

INT. A THEATER - NIGHT

A placard in the lobby of a small downtown theater advertises a play called *Dog's Life*. Richard and Cynthia are seated inside, as the lights go down and several dogs walk on stage, more or less choreographed, and begin BARKING.

                    CYNTHIA
                  (whispering)
It's an experimental work exploring the relationship between mankind's search for God and his baser animal instincts.

                    RICHARD
                  (whispering)
But they're dogs.

                    CYNTHIA
The playwright has chosen the dog—i.e., "God" spelled backwards—to symbolize the fundamental contradiction at the core of human existence. He's trying to capture the essence of mankind's very "dogness," as it were, by focusing on the dog's true inner self—the place out of which he exists as a dog...

                    RICHARD
I can't believe we paid $40 to watch a bunch of dogs barking.

A MAN sitting in front of them whirls around.

                    MAN
Shh! I can't hear!

INT. A CAR - NIGHT

Richard sits in the passenger seat of Darcy Myers's Subaru, tensely gripping the dashboard as she darts through downtown traffic. Her car is a repository for balled-up Kleenex.

                    DARCY
If you don't want to go out with me again,

that's okay. I'll understand. I mean, it's not like I'm still suicidal.

> RICHARD
> Have you ever had an accident?

> DARCY
> Well, that depends on your definition of an accident.

> RICHARD
> Huh?

> DARCY
> As far as I'm concerned, it doesn't count as an accident unless it involves flashing lights and people in uniforms. So technically, no, I've never had an accident.

Richard doesn't look reassured.

INT. A BEDROOM - NIGHT

Betsy is lying flat on her back, her face impassive, headphones strapped to her head, listening to a foreign-language instruction tape, while Richard tries to make love to her.

> VOICE ON TAPE
> The cat is in the tree. Le chat est dans l'arbre.

> BETSY
> Le chat est dans l'arbre.

> VOICE ON TAPE
> Le chat est dans l'arbre.

                    BETSY
          Le chat est dans l'arbre.

                VOICE ON TAPE
          Which way to the jai alai fronton? Où est le
          fronton?

                    BETSY
          Où est le fronton?

INT. THE VIDEO STORE - DAY

Richard listlessly waits on customers one after another.

                RICHARD (V.O.)
          God, what am I still doing here? Precious
          seconds are slipping away. I want to be on
          The Tonight Show. I want to burn myself
          into human memory and make them wear
          me like a scar. Sometimes I just want to
          disappear.

Richard vanishes.

EXT. WILDERNESS - DAY

With his arms outstretched and the wind in his face, Richard is flying, literally—over rolling hills and grassy plains and herds of antelope, he soars like a glider, free at last. Suddenly, Richard feels a jolt. Someone has lassoed a rope to his leg—a tiny figure far below. It's Mr. Pearson, yanking the rope with all his might and skittering across the ground like someone wrestling a runaway kite. Richard flaps his arms to escape, but it's hopeless and he tumbles out of the sky.

INT. THE VIDEO STORE - DAY

Richard is besieged by angry CUSTOMERS.

> WOMAN #1
> This isn't what I asked for.

> WOMAN #2
> $3.98? That's not what I paid last time!

> WOMAN #1
> Excuse me! You gave me the wrong tape!

> MAN
> I'm really in a hurry. Could we speed things up here?

> WOMAN #2
> I'm not paying $3.98!

> WOMAN #1
> I asked for *Terminator 2*; you gave me *Terminator 1*!

Richard brusquely exchanges her tape.

> RICHARD
> (under his breath)
> Like it makes a difference.

> RICHARD (V.O.)
> Make them wait. Make them beg for it.

A MAN cuts to the front of the line and throws his money and videotape on the counter with a snort of impatience.

                    MAN
            Excuse me! I have a train to catch.

He hurries for the door as Richard tries to catch the money and watches the tape slide to the floor.

                    RICHARD
                   (sarcastic)
            Oh, thank you very much, sir—I'm not a
            goddamn dog!

Richard SLAMS the cash drawer closed and wanders away to the TV set, leaving a line of angry customers behind him. Mr. Pearson pokes his head out the office door to investigate.

                    MR. PEARSON
            Richard, can I talk to you, please? Now.

Richard walks toward the office.

                    RICHARD (V.O.)
            Go ahead. Fire me. I dare you.

INT. RICHARD'S APARTMENT - NIGHT

Richard sits in front of the television, eating from a carton of ice cream.

                    RICHARD (V.O.)
            Whenever you're fired from a job, you
            should take something home with you, a
            little memento.

Surrounding the television are towering stacks of videotapes. A new VCR is playing a movie.

INT. A DEPARTMENT STORE - DAY

Wearing a loose jacket and a striped shirt, Richard browses self-consciously through a rack of clothing.

> RICHARD (V.O.)
> Pick a day when it's busy and you can lose yourself in the crowd. Stick with large stores staffed by sullen teenagers.

He glances at a SALES CLERK folding clothes; ANOTHER is working at the register. He glimpses himself in a circular security mirror hanging in the corner and quickly slides out of view.

> RICHARD (V.O.) (cont.)
> Never hit the same store twice in one week. Check for cameras and know your angles; seek out the store's blind spots. Stripes are helpful in concealing merchandise.

He picks up a folded shirt and passes behind a pillar. When he reappears, the shirt is gone and Richard heads for the door.

> RICHARD (V.O.)
> Above all, cultivate a sense of paranoia. The best shoplifter in the world is the one who assumes that everyone is watching him.

INT. RICHARD'S APARTMENT - NIGHT

Richard stands before a full-length mirror, practicing the art of sliding objects into his jacket in one smooth motion.

> RICHARD (V.O.)
> No matter how many times you practice at home, nothing can prepare you for that rush of fear and excitement.

INT. A BOOKSTORE - DAY

Richard browses through the aisles.

> RICHARD (V.O.)
> Shoplifting announces your presence to the world. It says, "I am here. I exist. I am free to do as I please. You can't take me for granted."

With trembling hands and face flush with excitement, Richard slips a book into his jacket and heads for the exit.

INT. RICHARD'S APARTMENT - NIGHT

Richard's apartment has been transformed into a veritable warehouse: Stacks of brand-new hardcover books and audio cassettes compete for space with sunglasses and clock radios, a multicolored assortment of candles, a row of empty picture frames, a pile of oxford button-down shirts. In the corner, a cluster of fire extinguishers sprout like blazing cacti; on the wall, a huge photograph of an eye.

> RICHARD (V.O.)
> Once you start, it becomes an addiction. You crave that rush, that feeling of power. The feeling of no longer being a victim. The feeling that anything is possible now.

INT. A COLLEGE LIBRARY - DAY

Shelving books at his new job, Richard peers through a crack in the shelves at KAREN at work behind the circulation desk. She's attractive in a mousy, librarianish way.

> RICHARD (V.O.)
> Her name is Karen Ryan. She's a part-time

library assistant studying art history. I've been watching her since I started here. She's originally from Pittsburgh. Her birthday is May 27th. She likes penguins and the color blue. This morning she brushed up against me in Reference. And again when I was coming back from lunch. That's too often for it to be just an accident.... Wait.

Richard watches the LIBRARIAN talking to Karen.

LIBRARIAN
Karen, I'm heading out for a few minutes. Can you hold the fort?

KAREN
Sure.

The librarian leaves and Karen is left alone at the desk.

RICHARD (V.O.)
This is it. Oh God, what should I say? Come on, think! You don't have much time. Go, just go!

His heart audibly POUNDING, Richard approaches in SLOW MOTION. He imagines taking Karen in his arms and kissing her passionately.

CUT TO: The wedding. Richard and Karen take their vows in the library's atrium.

CUT TO: The honeymoon. A SHIP'S HORN blows and confetti flies as they stand against the railing of the library's balcony as if it were a cruise ship.

CUT TO: Richard and Karen holding their new BABY.

CUT TO: Richard approaching Karen. She smiles at him and his gaze wanders bizarrely, desperately trying to avoid eye contact.

> KAREN
>
> Hi.

> RICHARD
>
> Hi... I– uh...

Richard seems ready to pass out.

EXT. A MOVIE THEATER - NIGHT

Holding a hastily wrapped package, Richard waits as Karen approaches.

> RICHARD (V.O.)
>
> I can't believe she said yes. God, I'm so nervous.

> KAREN
> *(breathless)*
>
> Hi! I thought I was going to be late.

> RICHARD
>
> No, we still have a few minutes.... I–um, I got this for you.

He hands her the package.

> KAREN
>
> Oh, you shouldn't have done that.

She starts to open it.

                    RICHARD
            Sorry it looks like it was wrapped by mon-
            keys.

It's a stuffed penguin.

                    KAREN
            Oh, thank you! That's so sweet.

She touches his arm in thanks.

                    RICHARD
            Well, secretly I'm a nice guy. Don't tell
            anyone, though—you'll blow my cover.

She laughs as they enter the theater together.

INT. THE MOVIE THEATER - NIGHT

Richard and Karen are sitting together with a box of popcorn, watching the movie. Richard's body is rigid with fear as he peeks at her out of the corner of his eye.

                    RICHARD (V.O.)
            The scent of her hair, the rustle of her
            clothing, the fresh recent-shower smell of
            her skin.... I can feel the heat of her body
            beside me. In the darkness, I start to ideal-
            ize her features just enough to imagine
            she's beautiful, to imagine her smooth
            white legs beneath that coarse librarian's
            skirt....

She crosses her legs and her knee brushes against his, sending a jolt of electricity through his body. Richard finally gets up the nerve to slip his arm around the back of her seat and let it fall lightly, as if by accident, onto her shoulder.

> RICHARD (V.O.) (cont.)
> I can feel the muscles beneath her sweater tighten ever so slightly, but she doesn't resist... and I'm in heaven.

He doesn't look like he's in heaven. He looks like he's about to be wheeled into surgery.

EXT. A CITY SIDEWALK - NIGHT

Strolling along the sidewalk, Richard and Karen stop in front of her apartment building and face each other awkwardly.

> KAREN
> Well... this is it.

> RICHARD
> This is it.

> KAREN
> Um, thanks a lot. I had a really good time.

> RICHARD (V.O.)
> If you knew how much I loved you, you'd faint.

> RICHARD
> Oh, uh... you're welcome.

> RICHARD (V.O.)
> Kiss her! No, wait!! Okay, now. No! Yes! Now, do it now!

                    KAREN
    Well, good night.

                    RICHARD
    Good night.

She turns, unlocks the door, and disappears inside, as Richard stares after her achingly.

                    RICHARD (V.O.)
    I will not fall in love with her. I will not fall
    in love with her. I'll keep my heart on a
    leash if I have to, but I won't let it drag me
    down again.

INT. THE LIBRARY - DAY

Richard pushes a cart through the stacks, shelving books and watching the STUDENTS studying in their carrels.

                    RICHARD (V.O.)
    Every day you give them a portion of your
    life and they give you a paycheck. The only
    life you'll ever get, and you just sell it for
    cash, one piece at a time.... There has to be
    something more.

Richard catches a fleeting glimpse of a brooding, unshaven bear of a man, EDDIE BATISTA, pushing a book cart like his. He watches with curiosity and dread, but Eddie quickly averts his gaze and vanishes into the stacks.

INT. THE LIBRARY - DAY

Richard spies on Karen through a crack in the shelves and approaches her as soon as she's alone at the desk, busily filing shelf cards.

                    RICHARD
Hi, Karen.

                    KAREN
              (preoccupied)
Oh, hi, uh... Richard.

                    RICHARD
It's been really busy today. Must be finals, I guess.

                    KAREN
Huh? Yeah.

                    RICHARD
    (desperately trying to make conversation)
That was some movie the other night.

                    KAREN
Yeah, pretty bad.

                    RICHARD
Yeah. Good, uh, seats, though.

He rolls his eyes.

                    RICHARD (cont.)
I always try to sit so I'm as far from the screen as the screen is wide. I find that to be the, uh, optimal distance.

                    KAREN
Oh? I never really thought of that.

                    RICHARD
Yeah.... I was thinking of going out to din-

ner tomorrow and I was wondering if you'd like to, uh... you know, if– if you—

KAREN
Oh, that's really sweet of you, but I'm so busy with exams and everything, it's really hard—

RICHARD
Oh, I understand, it's no big—

KAREN
Maybe some other time.

RICHARD
Oh, sure. Yeah, okay.

Richard slinks back to work.

RICHARD (V.O.)
Too soon—I should've waited. Stupid!

INT. THE LIBRARY - NIGHT

Richard locks the front door for the night and starts turning off the lights. His FOOTSTEPS echo through the cavernous, eerily silent building. Suddenly he stops and cocks his head to an unexpected sound: a faint ELECTRONIC SQUEAL. He walks slowly from room to room, trying to pinpoint its source, finally stopping at a rarely used staircase leading into the basement. He switches on a dusty bulb and descends into the darkness.

INT. A STORAGE ROOM - NIGHT

Richard flicks on a light to reveal a dark forest of old bookcases. He wanders through the narrow aisles, trying to locate what has become a REVERBERATING HOWL. Finally he steps through the half-open door of a long-abandoned men's room and warily peaks into a stall. Seated high on the tank is Eddie Batista, whaling on an electric guitar. He stops suddenly, startled by Richard, his last note echoing off the linoleum.

                  EDDIE
    Oh... sorry. Did you need to use the—?

                RICHARD
    No, I was just— I mean, the library's closing
    and...

Eddie glances at his watch.

                  EDDIE
    Oh, shit. I lost track of time. Thanks.

He jumps off the toilet, collects his equipment, and maneuvers his massive form out the door before Richard, bewildered, can say anything.

INT. THE LIBRARY - DAY

Standing at the circulation counter, checking out books to a PATRON, Richard glances furtively at Karen working at a desk a short distance away.

                RICHARD
    They're due back in three weeks.

He absentmindedly hands over the books, takes a deep breath, and slides up to her desk.

             RICHARD (cont.)
  Hi.

                    KAREN
Hi, Richard.

                    RICHARD
Um, I know you're probably busy, but I got these free tickets to a new club downtown, and I thought, you know, maybe, if you'd like to...

                    KAREN
Well...

                    RICHARD
It's okay if you don't want to—I mean, I got them for free, so it's not like—

                    KAREN
Richard, you're really nice, and I don't want to hurt your feelings...

                    RICHARD (V.O.)
Oh, God.

                    KAREN
...but I can't really get involved in anything right now. If I wasn't so busy with school and work, things might be different....

                    RICHARD (V.O.)
Here it comes.

                    KAREN
...We can still be friends.

The sound of a HEAVY IRON DOOR CLANGING shut.

                    RICHARD
          Sure, okay.

Richard walks glumly back to the counter, as Karen greets an
ELDERLY MAN approaching with an armload of books.

                    KAREN
          Hi, Dr. Brownlow. Richard, I'll be back in
          a minute.

Richard nods as she heads into the stacks, then he sullenly
checks out the professor's books.

                    RICHARD (V.O.)
          I don't care. I am beyond the pale of hu-
          manity. I am stark raving Elvis. Rebel with-
          out pause. I am Rudimentary Man. I am
          Johnny Death.

                    RICHARD
          They're due back in three weeks.

                    DR. BROWNLOW
                       (haughtily)
          I know when they're due! I've been coming
          to this library for twenty-three years. You
          don't have to remind me every single time.
          Just give me my card, please.

                    RICHARD
          I— I gave it to you.

                    DR. BROWNLOW
          You most certainly did not. If you gave it to
          me, I wouldn't be asking for it, now would

> I? Don't tell me you gave me my card when
> I know for a fact that—

Flustered, Richard hunts for the lost library card, finding it under a book.

> RICHARD
> Oh, here it is. Sorry.

Dr. Brownlow grabs his card and stalks away imperiously. Richard stares after him, seething with resentment, then turns to the computer screen. Under the professor's name, he locates the section reading OVERDUE CHARGES and, with a glance of apprehension, changes the total from $0.75 to $7,500.00.

EXT. KAREN'S APARTMENT BUILDING - NIGHT

Across the street from Karen's apartment, Richard lurks in the shadows, staring up at the light in her window.

> RICHARD (V.O.)
> Sometimes I'll call her and hang up just to
> hear her voice.

The light goes off in Karen's apartment. Richard takes out a detailed chart, checks his watch, and fills in the time. As she comes out the door, he presses further into the shadows. Soon a CURLY-HAIRED GUY approaches, and Karen falls into his arms. Richard's eyes peer from the darkness, mournfully watching the two young lovers disappear down the sidewalk.

> RICHARD (V.O.) (cont.)
> I bet his name is Steve.... His name is always
> Steve. I've been having terrible dreams of a
> million guys named Steve.

EXT. A CITY STREET - DAY

Behind the wheel of his rented Ford, Richard is still stuck in traffic. The digital clock on the dashboard reads 11:42.

> RICHARD (V.O.)
> This city is like a tumor on the face of the earth. The rain doesn't stop here; it just goes into remission.... I've begun to appreciate the beauty of destruction. Sometimes I think thermonuclear war wouldn't be such a bad idea. The ancient Chinese worshipped the cleansing power of fire. Maybe that's what this place needs.

EXT. CLUB NEUROTICA - NIGHT

A sign announces the appearance of a band called Outside Agitators. Richard pulls open the heavy door to the grungy, underground club, unleashing a BLITZKRIEG OF NOISE. Light from a street lamp pours into the darkness, illuminating pale, expressionless faces dancing inside, all shrouded in black, like revelers at Club of the Living Dead. Richard and Darcy Myers descend into the maelstrom.

INT. CLUB NEUROTICA - NIGHT

Over a surging wave of sound, Darcy shouts at Richard.

> RICHARD
> What?! I can't hear you!!

> DARCY
> I said, let's dance!

She takes his arm and pulls him into the sweaty, pulsating mass of bodies. Richard shakes his head and tries to pull away.

                    RICHARD
            No, really— I— I can't—

But it's too late. He's been sucked into the heaving throng. Looking up at the stage, he's startled to recognize a shadowy figure playing bass guitar in the back. It looks like Eddie. Richard tries to get his date's attention.

                    RICHARD (cont.)
            Hey, I know that guy....

But she's absorbed into the crowd. Richard stares up at Eddie.

INT. THE LIBRARY - NIGHT

At closing time, Richard makes his rounds, first flicking off all the lights, then heading into the basement.

INT. THE BASEMENT - NIGHT

Richard tentatively enters the men's room and knocks on the door of the stall where the WAILING GUITAR SOUND is coming from. It stops abruptly, and he pokes his head inside.

                    RICHARD
            Uh... I'm closing up now.

                    EDDIE
            Oh. Okay, thanks.

Eddie gathers his equipment, while Richard lingers.

                    RICHARD
            I, uh... I saw your show the other night, at
            Neurotica. You guys are really good.

                    EDDIE
    Oh. Um... thanks.

                    RICHARD
    How long have you been playing together?

                    EDDIE
    About, uh, two years.

A leaden pause. Neither of them is comfortable in conversation.

                    RICHARD
    Do you work down here?

                    EDDIE
    Yeah. When they take old books out of circulation, I bring them down here. It's just part-time. If I get done early, I try to get in some practice.

                    RICHARD
    Yeah, the acoustics down here are great. You must really—

But before he can finish, Eddie has slipped out the door.

INT. THE LIBRARY - DAY

Again Richard is spying on Karen through a crack in the shelves, when he's startled by Eddie standing behind him.

                    EDDIE
    We're having a party tomorrow—the band, I mean, putting out a cassette—just... you know, a bunch of songs, and I thought, like, if you want to come....

                    RICHARD
    Uh... sure. Yeah, that'd be—yeah, I'd like to
    hear it.

Eddie hands him a slip of paper with the address.

                    EDDIE
    It starts at 10.

                    RICHARD
    Okay. Great. Um... what kind of— I mean,
    what should I—?

But Eddie has vanished around a corner.

INT. A SUBWAY TRAIN - NIGHT

Richard sits on the subway, brooding, on his way to the party.

                    RICHARD (V.O.)
    I can't believe I said I'd go. I hate parties.
    This is a big mistake. I should just go home
    now. I'll make up some excuse.... God, no,
    stop thinking so much. Everything will be
    fine. I'm all prepared. I've got my list of
    clever things to say I copied out of maga-
    zines....

Nervously he checks his breast pocket to make sure it's still there.

                    RICHARD (V.O.) (cont.)
    Just relax and be yourself.... Oh God, what
    am I saying? Relax and be myself? Now
    there's an oxymoron.

INT. AN APARTMENT - NIGHT

The MUSIC from the stereo is deafening. The PARTIERS fill the room with raucous energy, while Richard stands by himself near a wall, holding a drink and lamely tapping his foot to the music, desperately out of place. Every now and then he checks the list of clever things to say in his pocket.

> RICHARD (V.O.)
> So, I guess I'll just stand here for a while.
> *(pause)*
> Well, that was fun. But I bet I could have even more fun if I stood over there.

Casually Richard crosses the room, moving through the gyrating dancers as if there were an invisible force field surrounding his body. He takes up a new position beside a large potted plant.

> RICHARD (V.O.) (cont.)
> Ah, yes. This is much better.... Now I'll casually drink.

He takes a sip from his glass.

> RICHARD (V.O.) (cont.)
> Ah, refreshing.

Acutely self-conscious, he begins to examine the plant.

> RICHARD (V.O.) (cont.)
> Well, this is a truly fascinating plant. Really quite remarkable. Fine leaves.... I wonder how long I can stand here and pretend to be utterly absorbed by this plant.

CUT TO: Richard wandering through the apartment like the invisible man, investigating every nook and corner—the closets, the medicine chest, the refrigerator....

> RICHARD (V.O.) (cont.)
> Why do I feel like an extra in my own life? Like the main action is going on someplace else while I just stand here, filling in the background, without any lines to say.... I just need to find something to give me the impression I exist.

Still carrying his drink, Richard comes to a closed door; he tries the knob and pushes it open. The room is dark except for a street light shining through the window. Hesitantly he steps inside and shuts the door. A voice from the shadows causes Richard to jump.

> EDDIE
> How's the party going?

> RICHARD
> Oh! I–I'm sorry. I didn't know anyone was–

> EDDIE
> It's okay.... I don't like parties much.

A leaden pause. Richard starts to back toward the door.

> RICHARD
> Well, I'll just, uh...

> EDDIE
> What, uh– what are you drinking?

> RICHARD
> Oh, it's, uh... it's just water. I'm allergic to

alcohol. I just carry a cup of water so people will think I'm drinking and not—

> EDDIE
> Ask embarrassing questions?

> RICHARD
> Yeah.... Are you having anything?

> EDDIE
> Not tonight. They made me the designated driver.

> RICHARD
> Oh. Good. That's, uh— that's good—

> EDDIE
> Yeah, I guess, except... I don't know how to drive.

Richard doesn't say anything. Then Eddie starts to laugh, and Richard joins him. Eddie is sitting on the floor with a book.

> RICHARD
> What are you reading?

> EDDIE
> Oh, it's, uh... *Charlie and the Chocolate Factory*. It's pretty awesome.... How's the tape sound?

> RICHARD
> It's— it's good. I like it.

> EDDIE
> It's okay, I guess. It's not really my kind of music.

RICHARD
What's your kind of music?

EDDIE
I don't know. It's always changing.
(pause)
When I was a kid I wanted to be Keith Partridge.

RICHARD
Really?

EDDIE
Yeah, that was my big dream. Sing with the Partridge Family and ride around in that psychedelic bus. What was your big dream?

RICHARD
Uh, well, first it was to own a 64-box of Crayola crayons.

EDDIE
Oh, yeah, with the sharpener in the back?

RICHARD
The Cadillac of crayons. In kindergarten, the size of your Crayola box was like a measure of your social status.

EDDIE
I could never color inside the lines.

RICHARD
Oh, I always stayed inside the lines. I had this teacher, Miss Henderson, and she had long blond hair just like Samantha's on

Bewitched. I would have done anything to please her.

EDDIE

I had this old lady named Mrs. Stern. She had this disgusting flab on the back of her arms, and every time she wrote on the blackboard it would flap back and forth, and no matter how hard I tried—

RICHARD

You couldn't take your eyes off it?

EDDIE

Exactly! It was mesmerizing.

RICHARD

When'd you start playing guitar?

EDDIE

Well, I started on the piano. My parents forced me to take lessons with this crazy lady who wouldn't let you play on the black keys 'cause she said they were sinful. That's how I learned to love the black keys.... Did your parents force you to play anything?

RICHARD

No, but they were big summer-camp people. Every year they shipped me off to Camp Lord of the Flies.

EDDIE

(*laughing*)

Yeah, me too. I used to spend the whole summer locked in my cabin writing practice suicide notes.... So what do you do at the library?

RICHARD
Just shelve books. I don't mind it, though. I like creating order out of chaos. It makes you feel like God a little.

EDDIE
(after pondering this)
Yeah, I feel like that sometimes when I'm playing.

RICHARD
How'd you guys come up with the name?

EDDIE
Well, we started as the Embarrassment. Then we became the Splitting Headaches. Now we're Outside Agitators. It came from Reagan. Whenever he made a speech and protestors showed up, he'd always blame it on outside agitators. It's something authority figures say when their power is being threatened. I always thought it'd be a great name for a band. 'Cause that's the whole point of rock 'n' roll, right? Threaten people in authority. At least it used to be. These days the pimps have pretty much taken over.... It's like with the Partridge Family. Eventually I realized the whole thing was a sham—it was just a bunch of old farts in a studio getting paid by the hour. First big disillusionment of my career.... It's just frustrating, you know? Sometimes I still dream about being a big star and shit.

> Other times I just want to go on the roof
> with a rifle and shoot people.

INT. EDDIE'S APARTMENT - NIGHT

Eddie's apartment is as cluttered as Richard's. The walls are painted black and the room is lit by dozens of candles. His bed is a large inflatable raft, and a female mannequin stands by the door. Musical instruments of every kind—guitars, keyboards, a sax, a cello—compete for space with stacks of records. One corner of the room is a shrine to Elvis, with a life-size photo spray-painted with the words STARK RAVING ELVIS and a yellowed copy of a Memphis newspaper announcing his death. Eddie and Richard sit in front of the shrine.

> EDDIE
> ...on Mars, only 97 pounds. But if Elvis had
> lived on Jupiter, he would've weighed 648
> pounds.

> RICHARD
> That's amazing.

> EDDIE
> Every night before I go on stage, I eat a jelly
> doughnut. That was Elvis's last meal. It
> makes me feel closer to him. And did you
> know if you rearrange the letters in "Elvis"
> it spells "lives"?

> RICHARD
> Cool. Some people think he's still alive.

> EDDIE
> No, he's dead. I know 'cause right after he
> died, I was in a car crash. That's my *Self-
> Portrait with Fractured Skull*.

He points to a framed skull x-ray on the wall.

> EDDIE (cont.)
> In the hospital I had this vision I was at his autopsy. And when the doctor cut open Elvis's stomach, he pulled out a bunch of undigested pills and handed them out to everybody like Holy Communion wafers. 'Cause that's what he's like to a lot of people. So much of his music was crap and still he's bigger than God.
> *(pause)*
> Do you ever think about death?

> RICHARD
> *(caught off-guard)*
> Uh... sometimes.

> EDDIE
> All I know is, when I die, I want to be carried to the top of a mountain and cut up in a million pieces and fed to vultures. That way, when the vultures are done, little bits of me will fly off in all directions. I think that'd be so cool. I'm gonna put it in my will.

> RICHARD
> But what about, you know, not being around anymore? Doesn't that scare you?

> EDDIE
> *(awkwardly, after a pause)*
> Well, there was one time—I was about 14, and my brother and his wife had a kid. And they took a camera in the delivery

room and taped the whole thing. I remember watching. It was pretty scary, all that noise and blood and screaming—like Vietnam or something. And then all of a sudden the kid pops out, and he's all covered with this alien muck like some creature from another planet. And everybody's feeling all kinds of love and joy at the incredible miracle of birth and all that crap. But then, like, a few days later, the kid dies, and— I mean, when you're young, you think you're special, right? You think you're important. Like the world couldn't exist without you in it, like everything would just stop.... But the world didn't stop. I mean, everybody was sad for a while. But the world kept going. Stuff kept happening. People just— It was like he was nothing. A blip. Like he never even existed. And man, that scared the shit out of me.
    (pause)
I don't know.... Sometimes life can be a pretty poignant bummer.

INT. A SUBWAY STATION - NIGHT

In a dark, humid station, Richard watches a COP stretch a roll of yellow tape across the open door of a subway car. Inside, a YOUNG WOMAN is slumped in her seat, her body soaked in blood. POLICE DETECTIVES and CRIME SCENE INVESTIGATORS casually go about their grim work.

    RICHARD (V.O.)
Fear is the life blood of the city. The subways are owned by roving gangs willing to

> kill over a pair of sneakers. All they know is what they see on TV, and on TV almost everyone is richer than they are.

Richard turns again to the murder scene, only now he sees himself in the pose of the dead woman covered in blood. He blinks and the woman returns.

> RICHARD (V.O.) (cont.)
> When she woke up this morning, she didn't know today would be her last day on earth. When she stood at the closet and chose what to wear, she had no idea she was picking out the clothes she would die in.... Everyone stands on the brink of eternity every single moment. How can a person live with that knowledge and not go insane? How can a person live knowing he may never get to tell his story to the world? Everyone has a story to tell...

One by one, people standing on the platform—HOMEBOUND COMMUTERS and HOMELESS BODIES—turn to Richard and begin their stories, their voices overlapping.

> VIETNAM VET (V.O.)
> I killed many human beings on the orders of my government...

> WOMAN #1 (V.O.)
> We never talked in my family. We just taped Ann Landers columns to the refrigerator...

> HOMELESS MAN #1 (V.O.)
> It's so hot. It never used to be this hot. The

weather's been acting strange ever since they took them rocks off the moon...

                WOMAN #2 (V.O.)
Every man in my life has abandoned me. I can feel the world spinning under my feet...

                MAN #1 (V.O.)
Everywhere I turn, couples holding hands, laughing and talking, completely ignoring me...

              HOMELESS WOMAN (V.O.)
I ain't a drunk, if that's what you're thinking. My brain waves are being stolen by the Housing Authority...

                MAN #2 (V.O.)
I can't take this daily grind anymore. I want to tell my supervisor exactly what I think of him...

                WOMAN #3 (V.O.)
I want to buy a farm in Maine and make it a home for abandoned dogs...

                WOMAN #4 (V.O.)
I want to be a little old lady who bakes and tells colorful stories...

                MAN #3 (V.O.)
I want to start my own religion, with sex as the ultimate act of worship...

                WOMAN #5 (V.O.)
I just want to catch the first bus whose destination is "away"...

MAN #4 (V.O.)
I want to have it all. I mean, I want to get *away* from it all. No, wait—I can't decide!

A HOMELESS MAN wanders by with purposeful aimlessness.

HOMELESS MAN #2 (V.O.)
I want to kill the rich and famous and feed them to the homeless.

HOMELESS MAN #2
(to passersby)
Spare a dollar to play the lottery, sir? Spare a dollar, ma'am? I'm feeling lucky today. Spare a dollar for the lottery?

HOMELESS MAN #2 (V.O.)
Gotta keep moving or they'll think you're dead and bury you.

On the opposite track, the train arrives, and Richard joins the crowd waiting to board. A neatly dressed, clean-cut YOUNG MAN approaches, doggedly handing out pamphlets.

YOUNG MAN
Do you believe in Jesus Christ? Excuse me, ma'am, do you believe in Jesus Christ, our Lord and Savior?
(to Richard)
Sir, do you believe in Jesus Christ?

Richard looks him in the eye.

RICHARD
I *am* Jesus Christ.

The young man stares with his mouth agape. Richard boards the train. As it's pulling out of the station, he looks through the window at the young man and blesses him.

> RICHARD (V.O.)
> Frankly, I don't know if there's a God or not. But I'm slowly beginning to realize that I'm not him.

INT. RICHARD'S APARTMENT - NIGHT

Richard stands in front of his bathroom mirror, trying on a new persona.

> RICHARD
> Stephen Patrick Kennedy. Hi, I'm Stephen Patrick Kennedy. Stephen P. Kennedy. Hi, Steve Kennedy. Stephen Patrick Kennedy. Stephen P. Kennedy. My name is Steve Kennedy. Stephen P. Kennedy, so nice to meet you. I'm pleased to meet you, I'm Stephen Patrick Kennedy. It's a pleasure to meet you...

INT. RICHARD'S APARTMENT - NIGHT

Richard lies on his mattress, unable to sleep. The only light in the room comes from the TV, showing a newscast.

> RICHARD (V.O.)
> Strange thoughts have moved into the apartment. At night they sneak out and crawl into my head.

The television shows images from the subway crime scene.

NEWSCASTER (ON TV)
...Authorities are still unable to identify the young woman who tonight became the latest victim in a series of subway slayings....

RICHARD (V.O.)
A sudden event can explode a life.

TRAVIS
If a tree falls in the forest and no one hears it, does it make a sound?

Travis appears by Richard's side, barely visible in the darkness.

RICHARD
What?

TRAVIS
If a person lives and dies and no one remembers him, was that person ever really alive at all?

RICHARD
When James Dean died, the wreckage of his Porsche went on tour across the country and fans could pay a quarter to sit behind the wheel.

TRAVIS
Violence is always a man's first love.

RICHARD
The white marble tomb of Marilyn Monroe has turned pink from the lipstick traces of her fans.

TRAVIS
Will anyone even notice you're missing?

RICHARD
What?

TRAVIS
The end is coming; you have to be prepared. All those people who scorned you—you can't just let them get away with it. You can't let the world ignore you anymore. Life is short, Dave, but death is long.

RICHARD
Better to be cursed than to be forgotten.

TRAVIS
Write your own ticket to immortality.

Travis starts to fade back into the darkness.

RICHARD
Wait! I don't know what—

TRAVIS
You are the hole at the center of the universe. You are the singularity.

Travis is gone, and Richard is watching campaign footage on television.

NEWSCASTER (ON TV)
...The president's reelection bid swings into high gear this week with...

INT. THE LIBRARY - DAY

Richard interrupts his work in the stacks to study a book titled *Modern Terrorism: Motivations and Methods*. He takes out a slip of paper and a pen and surreptitiously jots some notes.

> RICHARD (V.O.)
> (reading)
> In a culture obsessed with images of violent death and destruction, a television camera can be a most effective weapon.

Richard hastily stuffs some books into his backpack. On his way to the door, he passes the circulation desk, where Karen is working.

> KAREN
> You're leaving early.

> RICHARD
> Yeah, I'm taking a couple of days off. Thought I'd get a head start.

> KAREN
> I don't blame you. This place is dead once exams are over. Have a good time.

Further along the counter, Dr. Brownlow is livid as he argues with the librarian.

> DR. BROWNLOW
> ...This is an outrage! I've been coming to this library for twenty-three years! I always return my books on time!

> LIBRARIAN
> The computer records don't lie, Dr. Brownlow...

Richard passes his backpack around the electronic scanner so it won't pick up the books hidden inside and heads for the door.

EXT. A CITY SIDEWALK - DAY

Walking with purpose down a busy sidewalk, Richard is slowly engulfed by the crowd.

> RICHARD (V.O.)
> (reading)
> ...A terrorist can be anyone: a neighbor, a coworker, a stranger on the subway—anyone with a sense of powerlessness. It's not insanity or hatred that drives them, but fear of losing their identity.

INT. A DEPARTMENT STORE - DAY

Richard carries a shopping basket through the hardware aisles of a discount store, while soothing MUSIC hums in the background and SHOPPERS march to and fro. He holds a copy of *The Anarchist's Cookbook* and picks out pieces of copper tubing by matching them to the pictures.

CUT TO: Richard standing in a long, unmoving checkout line. Suddenly an adjacent CASHIER opens up her register.

> CASHIER #1
> Can I help the next person?

Richard tries to jump into the newly opened line, but SEVERAL PEOPLE rush forward from the back and cut him off. He spins around and tries to retake his position at the previous register, but the line surges forward to fill his vacated spot, and Richard is stranded in limbo between lines.

CUT TO: Richard still standing in the checkout line of a surly, zombielike cashier.

> CASHIER #2
> Next!... Thank you for choosing Save-Mart. Cash or credit?

Richard gazes up at the front of the line, and he's surprised to see himself, RICHARD #2—a more innocent incarnation—having his purchases rung up by the cashier.

> CASHIER #2 (cont.)
> *(exasperated)*
> This ain't got no price on it. How come you had to pick one with no price on it?

> RICHARD #2
> I— I'm sorry. I didn't notice.

> CASHIER #2
> Now you expect me to go look up the price for you, like I got nothing better to do?

> RICHARD #2
> No, th—that's okay, never mind—

She picks up a phone and tries to dial the intercom.

> CASHIER #2
> Price check on register— Price check on—

But it's not working. She SLAMS the receiver down and yells at the top of her lungs.

> CASHIER #2 (cont.)
> Ronnie, price check on register 4!!

The assistant manager Ronnie—the same Ronnie seen earlier managing the supermarket—stands behind the service desk flirting with a cashier, one of the supermarket girls.

> RONNIE
> Can't you see I'm busy? Go look it up your own self.

> CASHIER #2
> I'm not supposed to leave the register!

> RICHARD #2
> I'm really sorry about this.

She stomps off angrily.

> CASHIER #2
> Stupid.

As Richard #2 watches her go, he makes unexpected eye contact with Richard #1, still waiting in line. Startled, Richard #1 empties the contents of his basket into a shopping bag, cuts through the line, and quickly slips out the door.

INT. RICHARD'S APARTMENT - NIGHT

Hunched over the counter like an amateur chef, Richard struggles to assemble his materials: copper tubing and coils of wire, bottles of chemicals, reels of cotton, a digital clock.

INT. THE LOBBY OF RICHARD'S BUILDING - DAY

Richard opens his mailbox and pulls out a package from the Edison Chemical Supply Company. He opens a manila envelope to reveal his photo attached to an authentic-looking laminated press pass, along with a boldly lettered sign reading PRESS.

INT. RICHARD'S APARTMENT - DAY

The completed assemblage sits on the floor looking jerry-rigged and harmless. But Richard's apartment is a total disaster. By now he's accumulated more possessions than his tiny room can hold, and his mind swirls drunkenly through the suffocating space.

> RICHARD (V.O.)
> My life has gotten too complicated. It's like a mausoleum in here. All this meaningless junk is dragging me down like a dinosaur into a pit of tar. I just need to simplify everything.... Sometimes I pray for a tornado to come and suck up everything I own, snatch the clothes right off my back, leaving me naked as a newborn baby, free from all the burdens of the past. Free to start life over.

EXT. THE FIRE ESCAPE OF RICHARD'S BUILDING - DAY

From a fire escape, Richard dumps the accumulated junk in his apartment—all the books and tapes and papers, everything—over the railing and into a Dumpster.

> RICHARD (V.O.)
> Once I started, I couldn't stop. I felt myself wriggling out from under the deadening weight of words. I felt the way the sky must feel after a thunderstorm.... According to ancient Chinese philosophy, the supreme good is divesting oneself of all of one's best-loved possessions....

Richard approaches the railing with his TV set. He hesitates, then slowly pulls it back and returns it to his apartment.

INT. RICHARD'S APARTMENT - DAWN

Richard stares out the window as the sun rises over the city.

> RICHARD (V.O.)
> I couldn't sleep again last night. Watched the sun rise, slow and reluctant, as if it knew what was coming. It's the kind of day when anything can happen and usually doesn't.... The temperature is 65 degrees. Skies are partly cloudy with a chance of death.

CUT TO: Richard hurrying around his apartment, combing his hair and brushing his teeth, holding up shirt-and-pant combinations, trying to decide what to wear to the bombing.

> RICHARD (V.O.) (cont.)
> When a man stops caring what happens to him, all of his worries slip away. I'll never be Shakespeare. I'll never be Einstein. I'll never be Jesus or Moses or Elvis. This is the only chance I have. I can't let death defeat me. Each of us plays the leading role in the movie of our lives; no one can change the script. The voices inside my head command me and I do what they say, no questions asked. I mean, if you can't trust the voices inside your own head, who *can* you trust?

INT. A CAR RENTAL AGENCY - DAY

Richard stands at the counter with a package wrapped in brown paper, while a RADIO plays in the background. A CLERK checks his driver's license and types on her keyboard.

> RADIO ANNOUNCER (O.S.)
> The temperature is 69. The forecast calls for partly cloudy skies with a chance of rain this afternoon. But the president is hoping it doesn't rain on his parade. He's in town for today's campaign event, which is scheduled to kick off in just about 45 minutes....

Richard checks a clock on the wall. It's 11:15.

> CLERK
> Are you one of the Kennedys?

> RICHARD
> Sort of.

> RADIO ANNOUNCER (O.S.)
> ...We'll keep you updated on all the day's happenings....

The clerk hands Richard his license and car keys.

> RICHARD
> Thank you.

The clerk doesn't respond, and Richard turns to go.

> RICHARD (cont.)
> *(sarcastically)*
> You're welcome.

INT. RICHARD'S CAR - DAY

On the passenger seat is Richard's package, connected by wires to the dashboard. The clock reads 11:22. He engages the clock's alarm, places the PRESS sign behind the windshield, turns the ignition, and pulls out of the lot.

EXT. A CITY STREET - DAY

Seated behind the wheel of his gray rented Ford, Richard is stuck in traffic. The clock on the dash reads 11:40. Nervously he starts to hum the battle theme from *Star Wars*. Suddenly Richard slams his hand against the steering wheel.

> RICHARD
> Oh, shit. Damn! I forgot to set the VCR.

CUT TO: The traffic starting to move, but Richard seems to be lost. He squints out the windshield at passing street signs.

> RICHARD (cont.)
> 49th? What?... Shit, where the hell—?

He spots a line of police barricades blocking an intersection.

> RICHARD (cont.)
> Wait, there it is! Okay, okay... Just relax.

He tries to squeeze his car through the barricades, but a POLICEMAN waves him back.

> POLICEMAN
> Whoa! You can't go through here! Back it up!

Richard stops the car, digs out his fake press pass, and nervously flashes it at the policeman. He glances at it, then waves Richard through.

> POLICEMAN (cont.)
> Okay, go ahead.

Richard nods and swallows, then slowly pulls ahead. The street is a maze of satellite dishes sprouting from the tops of news vans like alien vegetation. Richard snakes forward to where a MOB OF CAMERA CREWS waits in front of a hotel.

With a burst of groans and cursing, the newsmen suddenly wheel around and hurry back to their vans. Richard watches in confusion, as a burly, bearded CAMERAMAN hustles past his window.

>   RICHARD
> What's going on? Did I miss him?
>
>   CAMERAMAN
> Nah, they switched the damn hotel!
>
>   RICHARD
> What?
>
>   CAMERAMAN
> They moved it to the Regis across
> town. Can you believe it? There was
> a another fucking bomb threat.
>
>   RICHARD
>   (to himself)
> A bomb threat? I didn't call in a bomb
> threat.... I can't believe this. Someone stole
> my idea.

The clock reads 11:48 as Richard turns the car around.

CUT TO: Richard again stuck in traffic. He taps the steering wheel nervously and hums the battle theme from *Star Wars* even faster now, as sweat pours from his brow. A city bus tries to cut him off and he angrily honks his HORN.

EXT. THE ST. REGIS HOTEL - DAY

A phalanx of SECRET SERVICE MEN and a fleet of black limos surround the hotel.

INT. RICHARD'S CAR - DAY

Richard, still about a block away, tries to weave through traffic.

> RICHARD
> No, I have to get closer....

Up ahead, on the opposite side of the street, a car pulls out of a parking space just outside the security zone around the hotel. Richard sees his chance. He aims for the spot, but at the last second a cab slices across two lanes and cuts him off.

> RICHARD (cont.)
> Damn!!

Now he's hemmed in by cars on all sides. The clock reads 11:59. Panicking, Richard opens his door to escape, but it SLAMS into the side of the car sitting next to him, six inches away, and he's trapped. He desperately tries to squeeze through the crack as DRIVERS behind him lean on their HORNS.

> DRIVER
> Hey, what do you think you're doing?! Get back in the car!

Struggling frantically, Richard manages to squeeze from the car just as the digital timer hits 12:00 and a tremendous EXPLOSION rocks the whole block. The car and everything around it is consumed in a fireball. The blast knocks out windows on both sides of the street, and Richard is thrown face down to the pavement in a shower of glass and concrete.

Amid the SCREAMS of PEDESTRIANS, the SHOUTS of COPS and FEDERAL AGENTS with their weapons drawn, the WAIL of SIRENS and CRACKLE of FLAMES, Richard stumbles to his feet and staggers down the sidewalk. One side of his body is singed and bloody. He turns to look back at the hellacious scene.

> RICHARD (V.O.)
> My God... It looks just like a TV show.

Through the choking smoke, he staggers away, as a METER MAID nonchalantly affixes a ticket to Richard's burning car.

SLOW FADE TO BLACK

> RICHARD (V.O.) (cont.)
> Sometimes life can be so realistic.

INT. RICHARD'S APARTMENT - DAY

Richard is passed out on his mattress. Except for a RHYTHMIC TICKING SOUND, the room is deathly silent. The alarm clock reads 2:45—but that's not where the ticking is coming from: A stream of blood runs down his arm and drips into a pool on the floor.

Slowly he regains consciousness. Richard's bloody hand reaches out and blindly gropes for the TV remote. He finds it and flicks on the set. The television shows footage of the chaotic scene in front of the hotel. The explosion is replayed in shaky slow motion, and Richard searches for himself in the crowd. With the press of a button, he activates the VCR.

> NEWSCASTER (ON TV)
> ...Authorities are still searching for this man...

A grainy close-up of Richard escaping the car.

> NEWSCASTER (ON TV) (cont.)
> ...believed to be Stephen Patrick Kennedy...

> RICHARD
> David... I mean, no, Richard Freeman...

> NEWSCASTER (ON TV)
> ...the terrorist responsible for today's noontime bombing. A description of Kennedy...

> RICHARD
> Freeman... Richard Freeman...

> NEWSCASTER (ON TV)
> ...supplied by a car rental agency indicates he's approximately 30 years old...

> RICHARD
> ...King of Free Men...

Suddenly there's a KNOCK on the door.

INT. A PRISON CELL - NIGHT

Richard is locked in a prison cell, his arm and shoulder heavily bandaged, reading a newspaper account of his capture.

INT. RICHARD'S APARTMENT - DAY

Richard lies on his mattress, drifting in and out of consciousness. The TV newscast is still playing, while the POUNDING on the door grows louder.

EXT. THE ST. REGIS HOTEL - DAY

Richard flees the explosion, as television NEWS CREWS converge on the scene.

INT. RICHARD'S APARTMENT - DAY

The scene is the same. The POUNDING continues.

EXT. RICHARD'S APARTMENT BUILDING - DAY

Richard carries his travel bag and his TV down the front steps and away down the sidewalk.

> RICHARD (V.O.)
> I'll stay in the city another six months before I feel myself getting too comfortable. Then I'm heading for California. Where everyone is beautiful, and no one ever dies.

INT. A SUBWAY TRAIN - DAY

Richard sits on the subway with his TV in his lap—identical to the first scene we saw. Among the PEOPLE on the train, we see Travis, Keith and Tim, Eddie, Karen, Richard's mother—in fact, all of the people Richard imagined he knew, all of them strangers, all of them expressionless.

EXT. THE ST. REGIS HOTEL - DAY

The scene of the explosion. The POUNDING grows louder. Richard's body is pulled from the car by FIREFIGHTERS.

INT. A SUBWAY TRAIN - DAY

Richard sits with his TV. One of the passengers has a portable RADIO tuned to a newscast.

> NEWSCASTER (V.O.)
> ...Once again, a massive search has begun for Stephen Patrick Kennedy, described by FBI officials as a 29-year-old drifter...

EXT. THE ST. REGIS HOTEL - DAY

The POUNDING stops. Richard's body is covered with a white sheet.

INT. A SUBWAY TRAIN - DAY

As the subway RUMBLES to a stop, Richard looks up to see that the man with the radio is HIMSELF, with a bandaged arm and shoulder.

> RICHARD (V.O.)
> ...Maybe I can sell a screenplay. I hear the opportunities out there are tremendous.

FADE OUT

www.ingramcontent.com/pod-product-compliance
Lightning Source LLC
LaVergne TN
LVHW051115080426
835510LV00018B/2046